The Backie Wash Hoose Sauna

~

North-East lives through memories and photographs

First published in Great Britain in 2000 by Aberdeen City Council,
Arts & Recreation Department.

Copyright Aberdeen City Council

All rights reserved.

ISBN 0 900017 52 X

British Library Cataloguing in Publication Data
A catalogue record for this book is available on request from the
British Library.

The Backie Wash Hoose Sauna

Contents

Introduction	i
Contributors	iii
Gracie Wallace	1
Jim Ritchie	11
Kenneth McLean & Ina Ross	21
Lena King	41
Mary Johnston	49
Hilda Youngson	57
Alan Findlay	67
William McHardy	75
Ted Munro	87
Margaret McKay	97
Flora Duncan	105
Emma Webster	113
Margaret Farquhar	119
School Project	127
Acknowledgements	135

A Note on the Transcripts

Introduction

For the people of Aberdeen and the North-East this book commemorates, through photographs and reminiscences, the last century of our celebrated millennium. This was a period of great moment for all who lived at this time and North-Easterners were no exception. Until the First World War life still seemed embedded in the 19th century but the drift from the land and the ensuing industrialisation rapidly changed all aspects of life. Warfare was no longer a romance but a mechanical monster ensuring death and destruction on a grand scale. With this war 'The Modern Age' had arrived. The 20 years between the First and Second World Wars saw the Depression and the Wall Street Crash. Unemployment, poverty, and financial bankruptcy were the human outcomes. However, the unsettled business in Europe would facilitate full employment after 1939 with the onslaught of the Second World War. After 1945, the opposing ideologies of the West and East and the subsequent paranoia gave us 40 years of Cold War. In Britain the National Health Service was created whilst we entered an unprecedented period of boom.

Radio, perhaps the greatest communicator of information, had already arrived followed by television, which at its best, became an unprecedented world wide informer and entertainer enhanced by instantaneous satellite broadcasting.

Around this time a new industrial revolution emerged, not with the clamour of machinery and molten metal but with silicon semiconductors and miniaturisation. That emblem of our age, the moon landing, heralded the computer age and with it a communications system capable of circling the globe in an instant. Such is the unprecedented rapidity of technological change. Now we have genetic engineering and probably, despite the controversy, its potentials will be progressed during our new millennium. Though poised as we are for the next 1000 years, we cannot envisage what that advancement will be, but should it be possible for humankind to proceed at a similar rate to that of the past century - we can only wonder at what might be.

Above and right: Marischal College 1900.

Facing page: Shuttle Lane off East North Street.

Contributors

Gracie Wallace

Jim Ritchie

Kenneth McLean

Ina Ross

Lena King

Mary Johnston

Hilda Youngson

Alan Findlay

William McHardy

Ted Munro

Margaret McKay

Flora Duncan

Emma Webster

Margaret Farquhar

Kittybrewster Primary School P6

Smithfield Primary School P6/7

Left: Ina Ross' auntie Bella poses on a Sherriffs Ice Cream motor cycle.

Gracie Wallace

Gracie's world was literally blown apart. The bomb that blasted their house in Torry caused her family to be broken up and distributed far and wide - possibly never to be fully reunited. To this day the family's twins have never been found, supposedly adopted by a doctor from Glasgow. The rest of the family has been reunited.

Gracie's lone struggle through various children's homes is both an incredible and poignant story.

<u>Right top:</u> A dynasty of grandmothers. Celebrating Gracie's great great grandmother's birthday (seated, left of the cake). Seated right is her great grandmother. Back row left to right are: auntie Janet, Gracie's grandmother, uncle William, Lizzie, Bella, Maggie and Lillie.

<u>Facing page:</u> Gracie, aged four

Trevor Davies: You got bombed didn't you?

Gracie Wallace: Aye, we lived in Causewayend, 17 Canal Road in one attic but I was born in Foveran at ma granny's.

Ma mither went out there for the weekend an' it landed up that she had me. It was the year o' the flu epidemic, 1933 and folk were dyin' like flies. Ma grandma had the flu, everybody had the flu except m' grandad and ma father.

It wis durin' the worst sna blizzard they'd seen oot there. My mother then took the flu and apparently she wis seein' flyin' horses when I wis born 'cause she was delirious wi the flu! I wis there sometime then we went back to Canal Road where I lived. I didn't come intil ma granny again till I was five then I came in t' go t' school, Causewayend.

Top: Gracie's grandparents, James Hutcheon and Mary Ann Hutcheon. He was a Pipe Major in the army. Circa 1900.

Above: Gracie (at the front, looking away) aged about five, with sister Olive standing to her left and 'Micky' on her mother's lap.

I loved living at ma granny's because at a farm there wis everything from kittens t' chickens. Granda used t' hod the head o' the horse and ma grandma used t' lift me on, those were the happiest days.

Well, as I say we lived in an attic until we got a brand new house in Torry. That was jist before the war startit. Kerloch Place that's where it was and you can imagine outa one room wi five kids in an attic and going to a brand new house, m' mother was over the moon. She visualised all the things she wis goin' t' do and she did it and it wis super. Us girls had a room to ourselves and ma brother had a room.

M' father was stationed at Lossiemouth and he was like a Sergeant who trained the troops before they went overseas. When the war started the wardens used t' come roond at night and tell y' t' pit yer blinds across for the blackout. However, we looked right oot on tae the railway station. There was the sawmill round the corner of Menzies Road. Ma sister wis only a week old and that night we went t' go and make the bottle. M' mither had made a cup o' tea an' she sez, "I've got an awfa queer feelin' - go an' tek y' sisters through t' the bed an' pile 'em on an' cover them up."

I can mind sittin' doon haein' m' tea (I wis seven at the time). She sez, "Now here's a cuppa tea t' you." And she'd a cup and said, "I jist be ben in a minute." Then she said, "Jist come ben t' the kitchen," and we didna hae a curtain in the kitchen because it was higher up so we didna need one. So jist be that, a German plane had followed the train in because the sparks would come off a' the wheels. We used t' see this in

Above: Foveran in the 1930s. The third cottage from the right is Gracie's place of birth.

Left: At Foveran, astride her grandad's horse, Gracie sits behind her cousin Robert. "Those were the happiest days."

the kitchen, well they dropped the bomb. Well, round the corner there wis one chap got his head blown off and there wis a mate o' ma mother's got four fingers of one hand blown off. Jist then we'd got intae the bed and covered everybody up and then the whole winda blew in, everything. The rooms, there wasna a piece o' furniture that hadna been damaged be shrapnel. There wis a huge hole in the landin' and y' could see the neighbours downstairs. The warden then checked for injuries but miraculously only my mother was scratched - but we couldna find ma baby sister. There was sheer panic and the warden went in and he couldna find her either. Well that made it worse but another warden came in an' far did he find her? Under the kitchen sink. She wis blown fae the living room inta the kitchen and under the sink!

Above: Gracie's mother as a baby, sits on an aunt's lap. Taken about 1905.

Left: Taken in the Castlegate outside Cornwall's the printers (now Voluntary Services and TSB) just before the Second World War. The boy who was to become Gracie's husband stands second from the right (back row).

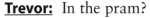

Trevor: In the pram?

Gracie: Aye, in the pram. It was miraculous that ma sister wis alright and naebody was seriously injured. It wis a miracle that's what the warden said. Well everything was wrecked everything had been new, we'd jist got out of an attic into a new home and now it was wrecked. We got taken from there and we went to ma mither's brother in Seaton then after about a week we had t' go to where ma father wis stationed at Lossiemouth. We then left Lossie and came back to George Street over the top o' Woolworths in another attic.

My mother had breast cancer so we were all put into the home at Linn Moor. Well I'd been in before and I was seven when I went in efter the bombin' an' I wis never out the hospital till I wis 12. I was at Cults Convalescent, I wis at Linn Moor Home twice.

Trevor: Why were you there?

Gracie: I was ill, I took rheumatic fever. Then I became ill after being bombed. I

Gracie's mother aged about 20. She died aged 36.

couldna tie m' laces, I couldn't feed myself I was jist like a person that's got Parkinsons. It was Doctor Esslemont who diagnosed me, she was the top doctor at the time. I was tied down to a bed in the Sick Children's (Hospital) because I was moving all the time and would have injured m' heart, you've no control over y' muscles. I got from Sick Children's up to Foresterhill and I had t' learn to walk all over again. I used t' get fed and everything was done for me. Be that time m' Mither died. I mind the first time she come t' visit me in Cults Convalescent, that's where they had the army when they were wounded an' they got legs off an' that sorta thing. It's still there yet. Well, she told me then that she had breast cancer. She didna have time t' go t' get it seen to, she had too much kids t' watch. It wasn't like nowadays y' could get fosters t' look after y' kids so she didna go to hospital until it wis too late.

When she died I said that I wouldna be goin' into any homes - but we did. We went intae Ferryhill Home but when ma father went down t' England he stopped payin' for us because he got married again so we got shifted to Westburn Road Home. That's when m' sisters wis all fostered to farms in the country. Freda and Micky, they were put t' the same lady and Olive and Peggy were put inta the same. That was at Strathdon with a Mrs Gardener. That left ma brother Richard and me. I went to Woodend because I was the eldest, I didna get fostered. I worked there but I got no wages from the Council. The only things I couldn't do was write and give injections. I gave out drugs, I worked in the kitchen, I did everything and all I got at the end o' the wik was a bag o' butterscotch pan drops!

Trevor: What, y' didn't get paid anything?

Gracie: No money only the butterscotch pandrops, I'm no jokin'. It wis, "You do this an' you do that." I did what I was told and with no pay. I was caged in there, it wis jist bars all round the grounds and I never got oot. I looked efter the geriatrics for about two years until I went to the Domestic School o' Science in King Street. When I got there I got paid 25 shillings, that's one pound and two half crowns (125pence). I thought I was rich but what did they say? "You'll have t' put that in the bank!" Miss Kelly, she was in charge of the whole school and I was goin' t' go through a cookery course and become a cook.

It was through a woman at the 'Dough School' that I met a girl who had also lost

This is the only photograph that Gracie has of her father (left), taken with other relations in 1935, when his eight children would have been quite young.

her parents so she wis in the same boat as me.

It was through her that I met my husband because her brother and my husband were best mates at school because they both come from the Castlegate. Anyway I got chums wi her and that wis it, I didn't look back. I met m' husband and my life wis great efter 'at!

I couldna spell or write so ma husband did all the form filling and that sorta thing and I did all the house keepin' because that wis what I was taught. I'd hid no education y' see but when I jined the school I was ae good an' I wis ae top wi this boy. We used t' hae competitions wi een another far used t' de the best and we always landed at the top. Remember the desks how they went up to the back?

It wis Glentanar that we went til for wer holidays. The Dominie and his wife they were very good. We went in a bus typ' a thing and we took our own mattresses. It wis the school at Glentanar we stayed at and we put our mattresses on the floor, it was a mad fortnight. It didn't matter how hot it wis y' weren't allowed t' go to the river. Y' were on y' holiday an' y' weren't allowed in the river! Ha ha ha! If y' did y' got a hidin'!

Top: Gracie, 18 years old and married. Photographed at 'The House of Fraser'.

Above: All together except the twins Brian and Dennis. Standing, Micky left, Richard and Freda. Seated Olive left, Gracie and Peggy.

At the end o' the holiday we got wer sports day fae the Council. The councillors came one day before we left an' that wis the spoon race, the sack race and that sorta thing. It was mair for their benefit - they could see that a' the kids wis gettin' looked after and the Dominie would tell them what was goin' on in the homes because some o' the staff were cruel like at Ferryhill. There wis always this girl who got picked on, her mother wis alive but she couldna look efter her. We used t' get sixpence on a Saturday that wis wer pocket money for the week. There was one week I decided t' go back t' get ma sister's ribbon, cause I had t' look efter the little eens. So I gid back for the ribbon, two o' them's hodin' her doon an' pourin' a jug o' water into her mouth an' she wis blue! My sister, the staff used t' pull her along by her hair. I jumped on the back of one of them. I couldna stick it nae longer an' she wis built like an ox but she had t' let go o' ma sister! I never got oot efter 'at. Mind you, we niver got oot onywye! Every night we had t' have castor oil and hot milk, y' had t' drink a gless o' that every night, codliver oil, a spoon o' that in the mornin'. Sunday night supper wis a little bunch o' grapes or a banana. They used t' tell us t' get up in the mornin', well we got up but y' ken what like it is y' try t' get an extra wee minty but they'd grab y' an harl y' oota bed. They used t' say I wis a trouble maker and if they did something to you there was no proof of what they did. It was only when we went on oor holidays and told the grown ups. I think that there were only two nurses that got the dunt because o' the lack of evidence.

Trevor: So you were in care there at Ferryhill?

Gracie: Yes that was at Devanha Gardens across fae the Church. We went to the church every Sunday dressed in we' bib an' bobs. They shifted us fae there to Westburn Road Home. 71 Westburn Road and it's still there yet. Some o' them were pigs - it wis always the little eens if they wet the bed. There was one, they used t' call him Pluto and I used to look after eight little ones from the age of two up to four. Y' were punished there, it wis the good old school strap. They used t' get a terrible smackin' if they wet the bed and Pluto, without fail used t' smack them. So I used t' get outa ma bed, go to the cupboard, get the sheets and double it over. We used to put them in the bath and it was always used for the wets at night. They were soaked and then laundered. That's how I used t' get the wet sheets out so the kids didna get a whackin' in the mornin'. It was always the same, it wis always Pluto, that's the nickname we gave him. It wis so sad 'cause I loved them as if they were my little wee brothers.

Kids today who are in homes don't know they are born but they didna dee the things you hear of now, sexually abuse them and things like 'at. We had neen o' that but if they were in a bad mood y' got a hidin'.

When we went on oor holidays we had a rippin' time because we said that if we were goin' t' get a lickin' we knew that somebody was there to see it.

After that I was bound to Woodend. My four sisters, Peggy, Olive, Micky and Freda were fostered out to farms in the country. They used t' scrub steen fleers an' that sorta thing; you've no idea the cruelty that went on. That was when they were fostered, it wasna real.

Trevor: What happened to your brother?

This was the last time that Gracie, aged 13, saw her twin brothers Dennis and Brian. Dennis' wee head pops up at the back whilst Brian sits with his tousled hair third from the right. Taken at Middlefield Nursery in 1944 the twins aged two, were adopted by a doctor and his wife from Glasgow. They have yet to be found.

Gracie: Richard went to ma dad's brother in the Shipra. The house is still there, further down from the Aberdeen Maritime Museum.

Trevor: What about the twins?

Gracie: Mother died when I was 13 and the twins Brian and Dennis were jist two. They were at the Middlefield Nursery.

They went from there and they must a went t' Glasgow that woulda been 1944/45. Instead of trying to keep us all together they jist separated us but we're all together now apart from the twins.

I got married and lived in the Castlegate so I saw Richard all the time because he lived roond the corner in the Shipra'. I've also got a stepbrother because ma dad married again so I keep contact wi him as well. The first time I set eyes on ma dad was 19 years after he married again. When ma Ma died that was the last time I seen him until I was married and had m' kids.

Trevor: What did you feel like when y' saw him?

Gracie: Jist empty, I felt we'd been abandoned. I mind the day they put us into Ferryhill and m' sister she sez, "dad, y' didn't give us wer sweetie." She meant the ration book for the sweets. He jist booted her up the backside and said, "Get!" That was ma last memory of him till 19 years later. I never had any feelin's for him efter 'at.

The
**Backie
Wash Hoose
Sauna**
~
Chapter Two

Jim Ritchie

Mr Ritchie's reminiscences abound with colourful anecdotes concerning that area of Aberdeen around King Street, Merkland Road and Pittodrie. Likewise his photographs are a depiction of tenement life in that area during the 1930s. There is a quality in these photographs which lends drama to the lives of the inhabitants. The powerful light and shade of these pictures combined with a humbleness of dress and an austerity of expression make the atmosphere almost tangible.

However hard working these folk were, austerity would always give way to cheerfulness as here below, when taking time out to have their photographs taken.

<u>Above:</u> The Ritchie family. L to R: Henry, mother Janet, James, father Henry and John.

<u>Facing page:</u> Jim Ritchie (with barrow) and two other inhabitants of 26 Merkland Road East, Mrs Birnie and her son, George.

Jim: I was born in 1917 at 26 Merkland Road East right beside Pittodrie park. M' father was in the granite trade and of course mothers at that time were at home. I had two older brothers and at five years old I went to school which was the one in King Street opposite Nelson Street. I did quite well there and I was always towards the top of the boys part of the class. I can remember the first day I was there with my mother. The other thing that I remember at the time when I was at the King Street School was when I was 10 years old I took rheumatic fever. I came home with a terrible sore throat on a Friday afternoon, sent t' bed, doctor in on Saturday. Unfortunately our own doctor was away and this was a character that was standing in for him and there was nothing remarkable in that he finished up in the Asylum. But he said, "Oh, nothing to worry about, oh no nothing at all." M' mother had t' send for our own doctor who was very annoyed and announced that I'd got a scarlet fever throat and it had turned into rheumatic fever. I was in bed for six months! The reason for that was for the first month they would try to sweat it out of y' then for the rest of the period the doctor would come in periodically to sound the heart and he would say, "No, you're not getting up yet." So, I was six months in bed. After that I was told, "When you leave school you'd best be a penpusher." Then I went to the Central School which is now that 'Academy' shopping centre.

Above: A picnic at Balgownie - 1920s. Mrs Ritchie, Jim Ritchie, John Ritchie, Nicol Carnegie and Wilf Shipley.

Above: Henry, James and John Ritchie with their mother at their home in Merkland Road.

One funny thing I can remember at King Street School was a chap came to give us our first lesson in swimming. We didn't have a swimming pool, in fact the only school that had a swimming pool was up in the Middle School in the Gallowgate. I remember our first lesson was in the gym and we got out those long benches. We were told to lie on them and start to simulate swimming and that was the only lesson we had in swimming! We never got to go in the water at all!

The first job that I had when I left school was as an office boy in a solicitors which was called Brander and Cruickshank. The one thing that I remember about that is that I got three weeks holiday in the summer the same as the other members of staff. That was more holidays than I got till well after the war! My salary was 30 shillings (£1.50) a month! This would have been the early 30s. I just ran the messages, delivered letters, went to the Post Office and that sorta thing. You were glad to have a job, in fact in those days if something happened you might get the sack and how would you find another job?

I eventually saw that I wasn't going to get anything there so I got into Middleton's mart at Kittybrewster. In those days there was no such thing as overtime. Normally, it was from nine till half past five but in the busy sheep season when there were big sales you were often there till 10 o'clock at night. You got no extra money for that. I used t' be in a sale ring on a Friday afternoon from one o'clock until the sale was finished perhaps at seven o'clock at night. So that was six hours non stop tryin' t' keep track of the auctioneer and the sheep. They could come in quite a number or they could come in singly so you were writing and calculating like mad. I've seen me doin' the other job and you'd be trying to calculate 13 times something and you'd have a farmer pullin' away at y' jacket, sayin', "Fans ma sheep comin' in?" We went t' the mart at Ellon on Monday, then on Wednesday we went to Maud.

Trevor: How did you get there?

Jim: We used t' take the train from Kittybrewster until eventually one of the auctioneers acquired a car, so sometimes we got a lift in the car. You always worked on a Saturday anyway but sometimes you'd be out to a roup. Two of us would be out there, no overtime. It was just taken for granted, it was a part of the job. It wouldn't happen nowadays. I used t' laugh at the farmers, they are still the same. A farmer would come into the office for his cheque for his cattle and he'd say, "Thrown away, a terrible price the day." Then you'd see the farmer that bought them and he'd say, "Far too dear the day!" You'd get the ones that didna pay their bills for maybe a few months, yet if they were selling they wanted their cheque right away. Human nature I suppose.

Where we lived in Merkland Road East the Students' Charities Week was very interesting. For the whole week the students would come round the houses or you'd see them at the end of the week on the streets and they were always dressed up. Y' don't see anything like that now 'cause they dress so strange these days you wouldn't know the difference! I remember there was this chap and his name was Ludwig. I don't know if he was German or what but he was a real dare-devil with the stunts he got up to. He went up the Mitchell Tower and put a skeleton up there with a bowler hat on it! Y' know the Rubislaw Quarry and the Blondin that went right across it, well he went right across it hand by hand. He was crazy but he always got away with it.

Although we didn't have the chance to go to the University in those days we were lucky with two brothers managed t' get through to Robert Gordon's and I got into the Central at that time. It wasn't till I was 40 before I gained a qualification to teach.

I eventually saw my job at Middleton's disappearing, being taken over and that sorta thing, and I saw an advert in the newspaper for mature students to become teachers. So, being on the commercial side I decided to go into the commercial teaching. Fortunately at that time they had just started the Commercial College in Aberdeen in St Clements Street down by the harbour. I was the first mature student they had. After a year there I got a bit of part-time teaching so that kept me goin'. I was getting more for part-time teaching than I would have got full-time in an office. I went to Dundee to do my teacher training. Eventually I came back to the Commercial College in Holburn Street and stayed there full-time for about 20 years. For the last six or seven years I was senior in the book-keeping side. It was a good move to go into teaching and I enjoyed it because you were dealing with more adult students.

My great grandfather came up from Prestonpans and he was a potter apparently, so he and this chap Gavin started the Seaton Pottery which was actually nearly on King Street. It was in a lane going down to the Links at Seaton. I think there's a church there now. A lot of it was making jars and things for oatmeal and sugar with people's names on them. They were presents for married couples and things like this. Apparently, my great grandfather had been older than the other chap and he retired earlier and this Gavin carried on for a time. Then when he gave it up another chap took it over up until about the Second World War and then it finished because he was down to making flower pots. Then of course the plastic came in and that was it finished.

Speakin' about grandparents, on m' mother's side my grandmother lived till she was 94 and that was in the 1930s, so she could remember back to the 1840s. She had all her faculties until the last couple of months. She'd eight of a family just the same as my mother funnily enough, and two of them lived into the high 80s so perhaps I'm a Findlater being 83. Life expectancy is longer these days but in the 1930s reaching 94 must have been remarkable.

My mother's people were Findlaters, her husband who was my grandfather worked on a farm at Loirston - that's Nigg way. When my grandfather died they moved into town and my grandmother stayed up at 3 Hillhead Terrace which is off the Spital up at some houses at the back.

M' father he was born opposite Seaton Pottery just off King Street, and when they got married they lived at 7 Merkland Road East which was the only tenement on that side because the rest of the street was granite yards. Then they moved across to 26 probably to get away from the dust o' the granite works. Speakin' about granite yards they had a terrible life working in those sheds which had corrugated iron roofs and apart from that you were out in the open. The dust was terrible.

Trevor: What was your father working on in the granite?

Jim: He was working on a pneumatic tool called a 'Dunter' but in 1938 he had to retire because he suffered from silicosis caused by the

Top: Jim Ritchie's grandmother, granny Findlater, at 3 Hillhead Terrace.

Left: Jim Ritchie's parents at Merkland Road East.

dust. He did get a sort of compensation and a weekly payment of some sort but he lived for another 10 years and died in 1948.

Trevor: How did he wash when he came in from work?

Jim: O, he just washed at the kitchen sink, y' just did the best y' could and managed somehow. I remember, but it might be a bit later, that the baths at Justice Mill Lane opened and you could get a bath there for a shilling. I think that would have been just after the last war though. I went up George Street when we stayed up at 'Split the Wind' and got the tram round and had a proper bath.

We lived in two rooms in Merkland Road East and the one which looked out onto the back green was the kitchen, living room and had a bed recess. The other room was the 'best' room. Well, we were through there in beds. It had maybe a bit of carpet but it was never used except for us sleepin', unless occasionally a special sorta visitor turned up.

Trevor: Did your beds fold away?

Jim: Yes, I had one that folded away but m' brothers had a double bed I think.

Another thing I remember about the old days was the washing. My mother would go down to the wash house the night before washing day. It was too bad if you missed it because of the weather. Six days a week, nobody washed on Sundays of course. You'd probably do some washing and each tenant had a wash day so it was too

Above: Mrs Duff at the mangle on washing day.

**Above: Mrs Ritchie and Mrs Whyte right standing.
Mrs Duff and Jim Ritchie.**

bad if it was lashin' o' rain. You'd put it up in the house somewhere. Anyway, she went doon t' the wash house the night before and put on the sticks and whatever to get the fire goin'. At six in the mornin' you'd have to go down and light it so that the water would be just right for about eight o'clock when the wash was started. You'd get the washin' out the boiler and into the mangle with the water runnin' down into y' feet and it might be a cold freezin' day.

Trevor: Did you do the washing then?

Jim: No, but I would have got a shotty of the mangle at some time or another.

Mrs Duff had got the mangle out somehow that day but usually it was in the basement.

In the winter they must have had to light a candle to see to wash because although there was gas in the building there was none down in the basement. The coal cellars were down there as well and the coal man would come down and open the cellar door and threw it in, y' couldn't see a thing it was so dark.

Trevor: Did somebody have to count the bags?

Jim: Well, I don't think that they were quite so bad in those days. Y' see, there's lots of things different than now. People, I think were more honest. Well, look at all the muggings that go on today. During the war we had a complete blackout but folk could walk anywhere without fear of being stopped and molested. You can't even go out in daylight today! You could just leave your door unlocked. I remember coming home from school and just walking into the house and my mother might be out visiting or something so the door would be open.

One time when we were kids there was a Gypsy caravan on this bit of waste ground near Pittodrie. They were often there and sometimes they were the old round caravans. Anyway, we were just playin' there and we saw that there was no one in, so we decided to have a look in, so we went up the steps and looked in. Then suddenly a tall bloke with one leg, a real Long John Silver grabbed me. Shakin' I was, and he took me round up the road to our house.

Fortunately for me there were one or two of the women outside having a chat at the doorstep. "What's happened, what's wrong?" "He's been intae m' caravan." I said that I was only looking and eventually the women persuaded him to leave me alone. I was never so scared in m' life! Ha, ha! Ha!

We used to get a board and four wooden wheels to make a cartie. There was a place out from King Street, a wee bit called the Bobbin Mill where they made round wooden things and they'd give y' these sorta wheels. Then you'd fix them onto some sort of axle and that was y' cartie, that was great stuff. Some of the more elite ones would have pram wheels and they were posh! Then kids would gather a lot of junk from the house and we'd put on stalls selling cigarette cards or something like that.

Top: All the women tenants at 26 Merkland Road East - Back, L to R: Mrs Kiloh, Mrs Whyte, Mrs Duff, Mrs Bremner, Mrs Ritchie. Front: Mrs Ramsay, Mrs Birnie.

Above: The team again at the rear of 26 Merkland Road East.

There was one shop in Merkland Road East at that time, just a general shoppie and we used t' congregate there, even on the darker nights because we had the shop light for illumination and we'd play hide and seek or whatever. This shop was the only one in the street and the trams used t' come out of the Castlegate or from the various places bringin' football crowds to Pittodrie. The chaps used t' come off the trams and come down past the shop buyin' cigarettes and chocolate and when they came out we'd ask, "Can I get y' cigarette photo Mister?" Then you'd swap them till you got a set. Then we'd go

down to Pittodrie and when there was 10 minutes or a quarter of an hour to go they'd open the big gates so we'd go in and see the last bit o' the match.

Trevor: So you were well steeped in football?

Jim: Oh yes, y' see there were three football teams at one time, Aberdeen, Victoria and Orion. They didn't get t' play further out than Arbroath or somewhere like that. They weren't in the Scottish League as such. My father played goalkeeper for the Aberdeen team. In 1903 they amalgamated to make the present club.

I did play a bit of football for the second XI at the Central so I wasn't too bad but when I went to work I always remembered what the doctor said regarding the rheumatic fever. Then of course in 1939 the war came. I got my medical and I'd say there were about half a dozen doctors and the first one was alarmed when I told him that I'd had rheumatic fever, so I assumed that I'd get a C3 but I came out with an A1!

I was interviewed by an army officer and he asked me what I was interested in and I said, "Well, clerical work of some kind." "Oh well, you'll be in the RASC and be one of the clerical staff." Within about 10 days I got notice to report to the Gordon Highlanders at Bridge o' Don. So, I was in the Gordons for three years. I did a year up in Orkney which, if you could stand that, especially the winter, you could stand anything. Then we were near Newcastle for a winter and then I went abroad to India and I was there for the rest of my time.

When I was first married we lived at 'Split the Wind' that was just after the war in 1946. We had an upstairs flat near the church in the corner.

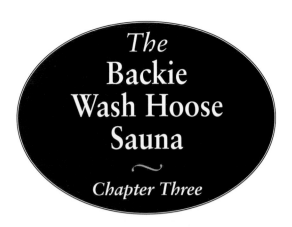

Kenneth McLean
& Ina Ross

West North Street and its surrounding area
provided the background to their early lives. From
the pervading poverty there arose in some an
indomitable spirit which enabled them to survive with a
quiet dignity and a morality not surpassed. Ina and
Kenneth were such and they exemplify that working class
stoicism through adverse conditions, often with light-
hearted humour.

Above: Kenneth in 1927 aged about 14 at the Aberdeen Middle School. Fourth from the left, second row from the back. Johnny Pattillo the famous football star is seated fifth from the left.

Facing page: Kenneth out walking with chums, 1930s.

Kenneth McLean: People were often very poor and it was quite common in my area of West North Street and East North Street for people to go to the pawnshop.

They'd take their father's suit or their mother's wedding ring or anything of value so that they could get some credit. Most people did it who were unemployed, those who had a steady job didn't need to do it so much.

Trevor: Where were the pawnshops?

Kenneth: There was one in Queen Street, one in Broad Street and there was one in Loch Street. There was also one in Commerce Street so there were a lot of pawnshops in those days. When they went up the pawn and got their money, they later went back to collect their clothes on the Saturday. The father's suit had t' come outa the pawn on the Saturday so that he could wear it on the Sunday. You had to pay so much pence in the pound to the pawn t' get your stuff back. Maybe a penny or twopence in the pound was what y' paid. There were cubicles in all the pawnshops and they were all packed on a Monday, mostly with school kids up with their father's suits before they went t' school.

I lived at 26 West North Street and the pawnshop was commonly used in this area; Chronicle Lane, Shoe Lane, Longacre and places like that. Now Longacre had no water in the house but they had a pump on the right going up. There was no gas not to mention electricity. They used pails for their slops which they flushed down the drain, human effluent, everything. Then they had t' carry clean water back up. There were two pails, one for the slops and one for clean water.

Top: View from 26 West North Street, showing the 'Corner Boys' (local unemployed) congregating for a chat with the attendant policeman.

Above: This shows the back of Marischal College. What is now a car park used to be a large grassy area. The houses to the left were known as Longacre and have all been demolished except for a part of the wall and the stairs.

Ina Ross: One thing I remember vividly is that opposite Chronicle Lane and where The Lemon Tree is now, there was a grocer.

Kenneth: Yes, that was at the corner of Longacre and it was Michie the grocer who was there.

Ina: Ha, yes Michie's the grocer. Well, I remember that shop being pulled down and I remember all the rats running from that place. I never saw a rat otherwise, you'd think that you'd see them running around the houses but y' never did, but there must have been food downstairs there. I remember seeing that from the windows of 26 West North Street.

Kenneth: Well that was all flattened out in the 1930s and the St Katherine's Club was built there, which is now The Lemon Tree.

Of course at that time TB was rife and people died a lot younger than they do now. They often died in their 30s - there were such big families living in one room, which was mainly lit by candles and oil lamps. That was in the 1920s - Shuttle Lane, Drum Lane, Shoe Lane, they were all bad and then there was the Shiprow and the Guestrow which was the back of Broad Street, where St. Nicholas House is now. Summerfield Terrace, Summerfield Place and Jasmine Terrace were a little bit better and tradesmen lived in those houses. Then you had Roslin Street and Urquhart Road and most of those streets were quite good. When I was a boy there were very few houses out King Street way, there were

This is Ina's grandfather and grandmother. He came from Northern England. He was a Garrity. The oldest is Tibby who died quite young. The boy next to her is Charlie, who once fell down at the docks and then became severly epileptic. He was never able to work but was often to be seen in Duthie Park sailing his model boats. Their father was in the navy during the First World War.

no council houses as there are today. Where the fire station was there used t' be a little park there adjoining the railway line. There used t' be swings and things like that.

There was a place in the Guestrow called the Dispensary where you could get free medicine if you were too poor to get a doctor. There would be a doctor there who would give you a line so that you could go to a chemist for some medicine. That was adjacent to Provost Skene's House. It was a voluntary thing and although I can't be too sure I think that doctors took turns to do it. There were lots of pends off the different places. Little John Street was another place.

Trevor: Where were the houses on Little John Street then?

Kenneth: There were houses on the right-hand side going up. There were houses so far up the brae, and then there was a place where they did armature winding for electric motors and that sort of thing. Further on there was a hairdresser, the owner of which was married to my cousin. At the top was the Middle School, that was the school I went to.

Littlejohn Street
in the 1950s

Kenneth's mother and father

When I was there an experiment was conducted on nutrition. So many people in the class received a pint of skimmed milk which had to be drunk every day, a whole pint. Then another part of the class had a pint of sweet milk and another part of the class had shortbread. Then we were all weighed and measured and got our height taken. This was an experiment conducted by John Boyd-Orr and he'd started this scheme, this experiment concerning our weight and height. After a while we got weighed and measured at various times through the session, and I put on weight and I also put on height. They did all this to prove that milk was beneficial to health. From that, children were given a third of a pint of milk in schools. That was the start of the milk for schools. At that time rickets was quite common, particularly in Glasgow, but by giving children milk, rickets was mostly eradicated. However, as we all know, Margaret Thatcher has taken school milk away although there was a lot more malnutrition in those days of the 1920s and 30s.

Outside the school was a playing field we called 'The Pitches', it was where the car park is in the Gallowgate. It was just a spare piece of ground and we played football on it.

Trevor: What did your father do for a living?

Kenneth: My father worked down at the boats, on the trawlers, he was a boiler cleaner. They were also called boiler scalers or scatchers. What happens is m' father was employed by one of the trawler owners and my father went down to the boats, and when the trawlers came in the boilers had to be descaled because they used salt water in the boilers when they were at sea. When they went away from Aberdeen they had fresh water in the boilers, but after being at sea for awhile they had to use salt water. The salt water then caked inside the boiler so my father had t' go inside the boiler and chip off the salty scale. Ina's father was the same.

Ina: My father was the last boiler cleaner in Aberdeen.

Kenneth: It was just a small hole that they got into the boilers. When the boat got into the harbour then y' had t' let down the steam right away and put out the fires. Then my father had to go in and chip, chip away and get off all the scale.

Trevor: Sounds a pretty awful job t' me.

Kenneth: Well, my father died young in his 50s. It was a hard job and the wages were poor. He was the charge-hand till 1926 when the General Strike happened. They sent up for him two or three times to come down to break the strike and he wouldna go, he was a man o' principles and then somebody else went down and took his job, so he lost his job. It was just casual work after that so he lost his steady job.

Ina: My father (Kenneth's brother) went into the same job but he'd seen what had happened to his father, he then took on jobs on his own account and he used to hire people and they would go and do the boilers for firms as well as boats.

Kenneth: The likes of some of these paper mills and factories, the boilers and flues had t' be cleaned out, it was a dreadful job.

Ina: When my father came home he was absolutely black some days. We'd no bath so he had just a wash in a basin, but you wouldn't find anyone as clean as my father.

Kenneth: What happened with my father and my brothers; Jim was down there at the trawlers working on the boilers as well. They used t' come home and go into the wash house. They heated the water in the boiler at whatever time we could get the use of the wash house. There was a big wooden tub and they'd take the hot water out of the boiler and put it into the tub and wash themselves there in the wash house.

Ina: Did my father do that?

Kenneth: Yes, they all did it. But if they couldn't do it in the wash house they did it in the house in the zinc bath. When we came in from playin' outside as boys we went up to the top floor which was the attic, and there we had quite a broad black sink with a tap which you could sit on, and we just went in there and washed ourselves with cold water.

After I was at 26 West North Street I was at Summerfield Place and there was no bath there either, so we went down to Hanover Street School. There they had spray baths for the schools. The children went from different schools to get a spray bath. On a Thursday and a Friday night I think it was, and a Saturday you could go in there and get a bath. It would cost y' six pence or a shilling and you got any amount of water and soap but y' took your own towel.

We were always clean and tidy, m' mother was never out of the wash house. She told me herself that the day that I was born she was in the wash house scrubbin' away' and she had t' stop to go upstairs and send for the midwife who came across. I was delivered and that was it. Most of the children were born at home in those days.

It was often hard goin'. Perhaps you'd go into the butcher and ask for what was left of the liver, the piping of the liver that were actually the veins, we called it a rig vein. We'd take it home and mother would put it into the pot and make soup with it. She'd cut off the liver and the dog got the vein. That and a bit of bread was your dinner. The only good thing about that time was that we got lots of fresh fish because father worked on the fish, so we got lots of fries. We'd have fish soup, we'd have fish fried, we'd have fish cakes, fish, fish, fish all the time.

Trevor: You used t' get fed up with it then?.

Kenneth: My father used t' say, "If you turn up your nose at something, sure enough, your other brothers will come across and whip it from yer." There was lots of soup made and there was a sharing - Mrs Londragon who stayed downstairs would send upstairs and say, "I've got a pot of broth do you want it?" and we'd share that.

26 West North Street. Kenneth looks out of the top floor window. Ina lived below on the first floor.

Ina: When your mother was older and I was the grandchild goin' about, I've seen her sayin' t' me, "Tak that wee droppe o' soup down t' Mrs Brown, she's just had a baby and she could be doin' wi it." So your mother did the same thing later on.

Kenneth: Oh yes, there was a lot of sharing, y' shared y' sorrows and y' shared y' wealth, although you had no wealth to share really, and your doors were never locked because there was nothing to steal.

Ina: You could leave anything lying on the stairs and it would still be there where you laid it.

Trevor: How many were there in your tenement?

Kenneth: There was one in the lobby and four on the first floor up. We had three rooms on the top floor. There was a living room, a bedroom and another wee bedroom. When y' went into the living room there was a bed with a table in front of it. There was a sink, a black fireplace and at that time we'd gas mantles. We had gas as long as I can remember and there were fishtail burners which I had through in my bedroom - our bedroom, there were a heap of us. We were head t' toe. There were six sons and one girl. Johnny, Jim, Joe, Alec, me, Bella and Eddie in three small rooms plus our parents. There were only four chairs in the kitchen so we stood round the table to eat our food.

When our father died we'd the bed in the room and father was on trestles in the coffin, and I was sleeping beside the body. You just accepted it but I asked the doctor, "Why is it that my father has died like this?" and he replied, "It's just the way of life." Father was just 54 or 55 when he died. He took a cerebral haemorrhage but he wasn't hospitalised and he was ill for about a fortnight before he died. That was in the November of 1934.

For mourning y' wore a black band around your arm for about a year. It was often a black diamond on your jacket, that was the custom. I had a black diamond stitched on to the sleeve of my jacket.

It was really hard goin' but we were happy, we shared everything. I've seen me coming home from school and sitting at home; my brothers were working at that time and they would ask if I was going to the pictures and I'd say that I had no money, then one of them would give me money to go. We shared everything and if you were stuck for anything they were only too willing to give it to you.

Trevor: What did you do when you left school?

Kenneth: I became a message boy for two years with a fruiterer and confectionery shop at the corner of the Back Wynd, where the taxis are now. M. and K. Gillespie it was called, then I met a chap from a baking firm. He told me that he was starting his time at the bakery and if I went up to the boss he'd be looking for a boy. So up I went and he said, "When can you start?" I said, "Monday." So that's when I started. That place was called William Philip and Son which was in Alford Place.

There were very few motor cars on the road in the 1920s, it was all horse cabs. There were no motorised cabs but the area was easily served by horse cabs because there were no real outlying areas like Kincorth and such like. Everything was within walking distance. I remember in 1923 when they did away with the horse-drawn fire engines which had a steam boiler behind which stoked up the pump. It was cart wheels that pulled it. I was nine at the time.

Ina: What I remember about horses was seeing a funeral, the horses with their black plumes and the driver of the hearse and the other guy all dressed up in their top hats. If it was raining they had black waterproof covers on their legs.

Kenneth: I enjoyed cycling as a hobby and on Saturdays I would cycle up to the Forest of Birse which is up past Banchory, about 30 miles. We started off at 12 o'clock because we worked on Saturday mornings and we did that from May to September. We left our camping gear with the gamekeeper so we camped there at Feughside. We went up to the farm and got a lemonade bottle full o' milk, homemade scones and a pot o' jam and we gave her a shillin' (5 pence). A shilling was a lot of money at that time of course, but sometimes she would give us a comb of honey when the bees were working. It was fine to get out into the country.

Trevor: What can you remember about your grandparents?

Kenneth: My father was born in Elgin and my grandfather was also born in Elgin and had a butcher's shop there. My paternal grandmother was named McKinnon and I think she came from Sutherland somewhere, she spoke the Gaelic. They came into Aberdeen and took a house in Marischal Street then took in lodgers. I never really knew my grandparents. When I went to see them I was politely told that they could not sit about speakin' 'cause they had work to do. My mother who was a Fulton was born in Poor Close in Old Torry. That's where those big tanks are now, but her mother came from Portlethen and m' grandfather came from Pittenweem in Fife. So it's quite a mixture. They stayed at Portlethen and my grandparents went out t' sea t' gut fish and m' grandmother smoked the fish at home. Then she put them into a creel and put it onto her back and then she'd walk all the way into The Green at Aberdeen and sell her fish. That was her weekly journey every Friday. There was no transport, no buses and there was no road as there is now, so they walked along the coast which would have been a short cut.

Ina's grandfather and his brother. He originally came from Elgin and died quite young. It is thought he spoke Gaelic and his family originated from the West Coast.

My mother worked in the fish which was where most of the women worked in Aberdeen at that time.

Ina : *We're a gan tae the Torry rocks, the Torry rocks, the Torry rocks, We're a gan tae the Torry rocks tae gaither dulse an buckies.*

As bairns we sang that ditty wi great glee, having in our time gathered buckies from the rocky shore near Aberdeen, boiled them, and poked out their succulent contents with a large pin. We were none of us ever sick after having eaten them that I can remember, so there is no doubt that our seashore must have been cleaner then, or our stomachs less sensitive.

Dulse, now that was another matter. It was a special delicacy; an edible seaweed that my mother would lay on the hearthstone until the poker, which had been thrust into the heart of the fire, was hot enough to roll across its length. The memory of the rich roasted smell of it sets me drooling yet.

Though a treat for us I was not to know then that the eating, and gathering, of it kept many West Highland and Island families from starvation. In our opinion the tastiest dulse grew out by the furthest-from-the-shore rocks, and as we had been well warned not to take too many dangerous chances with the ever-menacing sea, we preferred to buy our dulse from one of the fishwives who regularly stalked our streets of an evening much like today's patrolling ice-cream van.

Even in my young days the fishwives, in their distinctive black skirts and striped aprons, were like a people left over from a distant past. None of the town women wore anything resembling the dark-coloured, hand-woven ganzies the fishwives wore, nor did they drape their heads and shoulders with crocheted shawls.

Ina playing in the old stables next to her home in West North Street.

As they paraded our streets with their call of, "Buckies! Dulse!" I little realised that I was witnessing the end of an era when most of our North-East women, if they lived near the coast, would have dressed much as the fishwives did. All I cared about was whether I could charm a half-penny out of my mother or not.

Money was tight. My mother knew each day, to a farthing, what she had in her purse, calculating her financial needs with great skill and sometimes despair.

Debt was not our way. No, instead she struggled with her cash-flow problems expertly gauging when a halfpenny, or even two, could be spared for a moment's fleeting pleasure. Feet shuffling, almost holding our breath, we would wait her decision, and if there was a coin to spare you could hardly see us for dust as we dashed out into the street with a dish to bring back our purchases.

West North Street with Marischal College in the background. Ina's Auntie Bella (also seen in the photograph on pages i/ii) with Lizzie Clayton who sold dulse and buckies. She was never seen in anything other than fisherwoman's clothes and was one of the last people to have been a street trader who sold such things. The photo was taken in the 1930s

Weathered by the cold North Sea's biting breezes the fishwife's face resembled an ancient, brown, wrinkled apple with two glittering eyes almost hidden in the sheltering folds of her leathered skin. She seldom took time for a 'crack' with the womenfolk, and I suspected she had a poor opinion of 'toon fouk'.

While she measured out the buckies with a tin cup I tried to avoid looking at her calloused hands, so red and raw that my own ached in sympathy. I shuddered at the thought of how often on cold, frosty mornings she had thrust them into briny water, pulling my own hands back into the shelter of my cardigan sleeves as if that would save them from the same fate.

In the Aberdonian vernacular Ina Ross tells us not only her own story but also that of the common experience of tenement dwellers taking a bath with water from the wash house. These were the days before tenements were turned into 'proper flats' with their own washing and sanitary facilities.

THE BACKIE WASH HOOSE SAUNA

See my mither? Fin I wis a bairn her obsession wi' cleanliness hid me fair flummoxed. Apart frae the daily strictures tae wash oor han's an faces at ivery turn, the cairry on fin we wint oot onywye awa' frae hame hid tae be seen tae be believed. We niver got awa afore my mither hid bathed us an' dressed us in clean stockins, sarks an' knickers. "Ye'll maybe get run ower," she wid scold fin we girned that we hid been bathed a week afore, "An' I wid be fair affronted if yer underwear wisnae clean."

Fit wye she hid tae be sae pernickity fin ivery drap o' watter we used hid tae be cairriet up three flichts o' rickety stairs frae the backie wash hoose, I couldna comprehend.

Above: Ina with her mother in St. Paul's Street. In the background is the much lamented Co-op Arcade.

Facing page: Ina and her mother at the beach. This would have been a Sunday because they have on their best clothes.

A typical wash house boiler.

Fin I heard scientists speakin' o' "heavy watter" I windered fit they were on aboot. It wis a' heavy watter as far as we were concerned.

Washin' oor claes wis a day's wark in itsel'. Doon tae the wash hoose at crack o' dawn, even afore the sparras hid started coughin', tae licht the fire ablow the big biler which hid been filled laboriously, pail by pail, frae the wash hoose tap. Washdays wis the days we got second-day soup, an' were lucky if oor Mither hid a meenit tae notice if we slurped it or no.

Baths were anither maitter; only the littlest anes got a decent bath, for oor bath wis a sma' enamel basin that my mither wid set on the rug afore the comfortin' glow o' the coal fire, an' we were sat or stood in that, tae be sponged frae heid tae fit.

Later, as we grew too big tae stand in the basin we were left tae bath oorsels an' it wis a while afore I understood fit wye the grown-ups aye laughed fin we were telt tae, "Wash up as far as possible, an' doon as far as possible."

It wis a while tae, afore I understood why my mither, like sae mony ithers in these grimy, slum-like, city-centre dwellins, wis sae determined that we wid hae a' the benefits that cleanliness bestowed, fitiver the cost in hard work an' dedication.

We micht hae tae hale in ivery drap o' watter that wis needed, an' share an ootside lavvy wi' five ither faimilies, bit we wid be clean, free o' lice, an' scabs, an' ither sic-like naisties.

The buildin' we bade in micht be little mair than a hovel bit naething wis gaun tae stop the weemin makin' decent hames within its crumblin' wa's.

My mither wis weel pleased fin we reached primary school age an' got the 'privilege' o' a weekly excursion, in school time, tae the Hanover School spray baths.

I dinna think she iver kent foo much I hated them. The watter wis usually far ower het for a start, an' then, jist as ye'd gotten adjusted tae the heat, an' afore ye were allowed tae leave the shower, some sadistic han' wid turn the controls tae icy caul'. Bein' little I seen jaloused that if, at the first hint o' a drap in temperature, I flattened misel' intae the farthest corner, an' pressed hard against the agein', cracket tilin', I widna be stung sae sair by the freezin', sherp, needle-like jets o' spray.

Aince oot intae the dressin' room we were harried an' rushed until forcibly ejected, reekin' o' strong carbolic, half-dried, partially clothed, stumblin' in unlaced shoes oot intae the full force o' the blast aff the caul North Sea.

Since we were a' expected back at the school almost at aince, we slower craiturs hid tae dress oorsels as we ran.

Ina with her mother taking a pony ride down at the beach. This is the work of a photographer who was often in attendance at the beach. The old Beach Baths are in the background.

My school chummy wis aye dressed an' ready afore a 'body else an' it wis some time afore I learnt her secret - she niver dried hersel'! Na, spray baths were nae fun. I pleaded wi' my mither tae gie me a linie lettin' me aff gaun tae them bit I could hae saved m' breath. Ither bairns got linies, nae bother, an' I noticed sourly, it wis aye the anes sairest in need o' a bath that were let aff! Bit rescue wis at han'. My auntie Teenie got a bran' new cooncil hoose, complete wi' bath, an' we bairns were invited tae join oor cousins in the weekly bath-night ritual. Second or third han' watter it micht be, bit there we were, dipped, dried lovingly, an' set afore a cosy fire, a mug o' bedtime cocoa in ae han', an' a daud o' loaf an' syrup in the ither. Heaven could hae little mair tae offer.

The adults in oor faimily were niver oot o' the Beach Baths, eether showerin' afore their sweem, or, fin funds permitted, indulgin' in the 'Private Baths'.

Ina's grandmother, Georgina Fulton. She was from the fisher people of Portlethen and the baby is one of her children, perhaps Ina's father.

We bairns liked the Beach Baths an' a'. There wis this big communal shower cubicle which drew us like a magnet. Packet as tight as herrin's in a barrel, engulfed in a comfortin' clood o' warm steam, we blissfully luxuriated in the non-stop stream o' warm water.

Well non-stop that wis until some adult, frustrated in their attempt tae get a pre-swim shower, wid turn the lever tae caul. Oot we wid swarm like a pack o' steamin, half-droont rats desertin a sinkin' ship, only tae slink back ane by ane as the watter wis aince mair returned tae an even temperature.

I aye left the Beach Baths lookin' like a' stewed prune, an' it wisna wi' the sweemin'. I've aye thocht it wis the fault o' those seductive showers that I wis sae lang in learnin' tae sweem.

Fin the new baths were built in Justice Mill Lane it wis niver the same. There wis nae box-like communal shower cubicle there. The auld camaraderie wis gone. Ye canna huddle close an' cosy in a 'walk-through' shower.

THE DO IT YOUR SEL, FLITTIN'

Flittin' was another experience most folk encountered at some time or another and the not so well off resorted to any means to transport their worldly goods. Sometimes, if the distance was far or the load heavy, the hire of a 'cairty' from Cocky Hunter's was often the method used. However, an old pram would suffice for most flittin's. Ina Ross remembers times with nostalgia for those flittin's of childhood days.

Flittin' was a' an indelible memory for me - I hid a nostalgic pang for the roomy, but cumbersome pram which aince dominated oor twa sma rooms.

Doublin' as transport or cot, whichiver wis needed, it wis built like a tank, solid, deep-bellied, wi massive springs that widna hae disgraced a quality horse-drawn carriage.

Even if we could hae affordit the fare we could niver hae got it on tae a bus. Though I div mind that on one occasion, an emergency nae doot, the pram wis packet on tae the end platform o' a tramcar.

Nae that I mind on bein' a bairn in that pram, my memory's nae that good, bit the pram wis a familiar acquaintance since it wis handed aroon my mither's faimily frae sister tae sister. If ye werna in it ye were pushin' it. By some biological miracle my mither an her sisters aye managed tae produce their offspring tae fit the pram's availability.

This flittin' is taking place in Foveran and Gracie Wallace (see page 1) gazes off the picture. 1930s.

Nae seener wis ae sma cousin auld enough tae leave the pram's comfortin' depths than anither wee scrap wid tak its place, looking at first a thochty lost-like in a' that space. An' space there wis a plenty.

The pram coped easily wi ae bairn, twa toddlers tucked in at the haunle end, an' an assorted load o' faimily shoppin'. The pram's origins were obscure. I niver did find oot which een o' the sisters hid been the first tae mak use o't. Hid it been an heirloom handed doon fae the generation afore, or as I sometimes suspected, wis it a han-me-doon fae some stately hoose or castle? Naebody wis sayin.

Of course, as a bairn, I aye favoured the latter theory imaginin' the pram hung aboot wi priceless lace. I could see plump, down-filled silken pillas nestlin' aneath soft, lacy, wool blankets, an' toppin' a', a daintily embroidered cover.

In oor day the pram hid come doon in the world. Noo it hid a lumpy flock mattress, decently enough covered by a spotless, white-bleached cotton flour bag, cot sheets cut fae the strongest remains o' larger bed linen, an several multicoloured, hand-crocheted, worset squares.

It hid bit one adornment - an incongruous but beautifully embroidered satin pillacase, tucked in aneath the hood as if it wis ashamed tae be seen in such company. The pillacase wis an aberration!

Ane o' the fathers in a rare moment o' paternal pride, and an excess o' celebratory drinks, hid staggered intae Isaac Benzies ae day an' tottered oot again claspin' his dubious purchase in a glow o' darin enterprise. Aince the mithers hid stopped laughin' they agreed that the pillacase wis an improvement tae the pram's looks an' there wis much discussion on the merits o' buying a matchin' quilt cover.

While they were still discussin' the financin' o' such an extravagance, twa o' the littlest cousins took it in turn tae be violently sick a' ower the pram's contents an' the plans for the purchase were unanimously droppit.

By the time I wis in my early teens the pram hid sheltered its last bairn an' it lay, looking somewhat battered an forlorn, in the cellar, pressed intae service noo an' again tae act as a cairtie fin some heavy article or such like hid tae be haled fae ae place till anither!

Fin auntie Belle wis allocated a hoose in the spankin-new cooncil estate at Powis my father oiled its wheels knowin' it wid hae a few loads yet tae cairry. Belle's sisters, though a bittie envious, were ready enough wi their congratulations an offers o' help. While they scrubbed an' cleaned the new hoose the menfolk prepared for the flittin' itsel'.

No Shore Porters for us - the money wis needed for new linoleum, among ither things, so ivery stick o' furniture, bedding, kitchenware, dishes an' a'

Relocation 1930s style. Sometimes folk had too much and too far to go by pram, so something larger was required.

the paraphernalia o' livin hid tae be cairriet manually tae the new hoose.

It wis decreed that we youngsters could mak oorsels usefae an' be got oot fae under abody's feet if we were set tae ferryin some o' the sma articles fae the aul hame tae the new. "Tak the aul pram," my uncle said, fillin' it fu' o' pots an' pans, an' onything he thocht we couldna brak. We cheerfully delivered oor first load an' rewarded wi pieces o' breed an jam, set aff tae collect anither pram-load. I think it wis my cousin Alec who had the idea. The journey needed enlivenin' he thocht. He lookit doon St. Machar Drive which wis quiet an' deserted in those days, an grabbin twa o' the sma'er cousins who had begun tae get a bittie girny. He packet them intae the bowels o' the pram. Wi a wild whoop he set off at the gallop doon the steep brae wi the rest o' us streamin' merrily in his wake. We enjoyed that ploy sae much that aifter deliverin oor next load, since the wee anes, sworn tae silence of course, hid been kept ahin by their mithers, we took it in turns to crouch in the innards o' the pram on its downhill run.

The flittin' wis an evenin' affair - a winter nicht, dry an clear, wi an almost full moon beamin' doon on us as we laboured, takkin it in turn to push the pram. We werna feart. Cousin Alec wis a big, strong lad and we felt secure knowin that he wis controllin' the pram on its breath takkin charge doonhill. On oor fourth run oot o' the dark, like a Hound o' the Baskervilles, a black shape materialised and sprang at Alec's heels as he ran. His desperate efforts to kick clear o' the snappin jaws caused him momentarily to lose control o' the pram's momentum. It shot oot o' his grasp and set off bucketin full steam doon the brae. Wee Annie an Billie, jammed in the pram's interior were laughin' that hard that it took them a minute or twa tae realise that a' wis nae weel, an' their screams were added tae oor shouts o' alarm. The pram careered doon St. Machar Drive, accelerating madly until the camber o' the road drew it towards the kerb far wi a sickenin' jolt, it toppled ower, catapultin my twa cousins, luckily on to the grassy verge, an' lay upside doon, its buckled wheels revolving oddly.

Sadly, it hid cairriet its last burden. Nae collapsible buggy, fooiver well-designed or trendy could hae gaen an extended faimily sich years o' service, or pleesure. I wisnae the only ane tae hide a tear fin the pram wis teen awar on the scaffie's cairt.

Lena King

L ena claims a happy childhood. Her reminiscences and
photographs taken at her home at 88 Bon Accord Street
confirm this. However her father was killed at Ypres in
1917 when she was two years old. He was never found. Since
then Lena's need for some sort of resolution for her father's
death have grown over the years, with some consolation
through the dedication to him at the Gordon Highlander's
Memorial at the Glendronach Distillery near Huntly, and
through the newly located burial ground near Ypres in
Belgium. Through these photographs we can see the
movement in time of Lena's family from the Mid-Victorian
period up to the birth of Lena in 1915 then on to the Second
World War when she joined the Fire Service.

Above: Lena's granma' and granda' Morrison with her mother and two
brothers Benjie and Jim.

Facing page: Lena about one year old. Around 1916.

Lena King: My father was killed in 1917 in the First World War. He was actually reported missing but I found out later that he had been killed at Ypres.

There's a Gordons Wood up near Huntly, they wanted sponsors for trees to raise some funds. There's oak trees planted in memory of any soldier that you wished to dedicate it to. I didn't know of any grave or anything pertaining to my father, Private Andrew Hall, so I sponsored a tree. It's at a distillery called Glendronach - The Allied Distillers as a part of the Gordon Highlanders Museum Campaign. We went up to see the trees but we didn't know which one was mine and I've not been back since then, but it would probably be more organised now.

Trevor: Are they going to put a plaque on it?

Lena: As far as I know there is a plaque up in the Gordon Highlanders Museum now with a list of the names and where the trees are. I think there is a number on the tree and the names are in the Museum.

I don't know that there is a war grave anywhere but strangely enough I heard last week that you can find war graves on the internet.

Trevor: My son is on the internet I will ask him to have a look. (After 'surfing the net' a memorial to Lena King's father was found in Belgium not far from the town of Ypres where he fell.)

Lena: Well, you can take a note of the details. I only recently got the details because I wanted to find out as much as I could about it. This

(Ypres) was the actual battle he was killed at. The curator of the Gordon Highlanders Museum looked it up in the war diaries and gave me a

Lena's grandparents sit with baby Ethel. Her father Andrew is on the right with Helen and Dave in front of him. John, George and Jim are at the back.

photocopy. We had a cousin in the regiment who had seen him and that was the last sight they had of him. He was then reported missing after heavy shelling. There were so many dead, so many casualties and so many missing. I think he'd been about 23 when he was killed. I was looking up the family tree and he was born in 1894 I think. When you see those pictures of the battlefield it was just a waste of all those lives. He was in the 2nd Gordons and it tells y' that they were at Ypres in 1917. I don't know when he joined up but it was probably after I was born in 1915. My granny said that he did see me, but of course I have no recollection.

This is my father in his uniform before he went to the First World War. I didn't get to know him that well and I didn't get to know my mother either. She went back to Turriff to recuperate because she hadn't been that well. She'd been in the City Hospital and I'd been left behind at my granny's. I was then brought up by my granny but being so young I didn't know the details. I was happy at my granny's and the older children must have treated it as a novelty having a baby in the house. They were all very good to me. Nellie used t' take me out walks and I remember walking out with her on a Sunday. We went to St. Clement's Churchyard because m' grandfather and grandmother are buried there. Occasionally we'd go to the park but I used t' say, "Will the shop be open in the hole in the wall?" That was over in Torry and sometimes we'd go over there and that shoppie would be open and Nellie would buy me sweeties or something. The other sister was a dressmaker and she made dresses to me. So I wasna deprived but maybe they'd had a harder childhood. I did visit Turriff to visit my other granny.

Andrew Hall, Lena's father as a Private in the Gordons.

I was put on the train and they would meet me. That was during the school holiday and that sorta thing. Georgina Emslie was my mother's maiden name and she worked in Turriff for some time with my father at Forglen House.

It's an imposing house isn't it? This postcard must be celebrating the coming of age of Sir George Abercrombie and as you can see on the back my father has written home to my granny.

Trevor: Was this taken before you were born or after?

Lena: I think before because he looks very young. My granny used t' say that she'd give them all a trade, which was quite a sacrifice in those days, but she said that Andy was delicate so she got him into another sort of job so he could have been really quite young when he started there.

Top: Postcard of Forglen House which celebrates George Abercrombie's coming of age, sent by Andrew to his mother at Bon Accord Street.

Centre: The reverse of the postcard. It reads, "Dear Mother, I expect to be home for about a week on Saturday 1st. Andie. If weather is fine I will cycle."

Bottom: Lena's parents with a group of domestic servants at Forglen House near Turriff. Taken before the First World War. Andrew Hall, Lena's father is on the back row far right and her mother is back row third from the right.

Trevor: So your father met your mother there then?

Lena: Yes they worked together. He was a valet but she said he was a Gentlemen's gentleman who looked after Sir George's suits and she was a lady's maid. The rest are the domestic staff but I don't know anything about them.

My mother probably had a very bad time at my birth because I was born in a thatched cottage and it would have been very primitive, whereas I was in a hospital having my son with every facility that I needed. If she had a similar birth to me then she must have had a very bad time.

Trevor: Where was this thatched cottage then?

Lena: Claymires, I never saw it and I don't know where it was but it was somewhere around Turriff. They certainly didna live there when I went to see m' granny later on but they were living in a croft somewhere where m' grandfather was looking after pigs. It was a lovely cottage with a beautiful garden. He used t' say, "Don't pick the flowers out of the garden jist go t' the fields." So I always came back with wildflowers and I remember my granny saying, "She's been in the cow park today she's got tansys!"

Lena aged about two.

That's me standing on that chair, I was maybe two or even younger at the time. I was born in 1915.

Family photogragh taken at 88 Bon Accord Street with Lena at the front in the pale dress.

From the right Ina, Ethel, Helen and Catherine, and the three boys Robert, William and Edward. Catherine was m' granny's name as well. Although she was my granny I never referred to her as such because to me she was my mother and I didn't know any different.

Trevor: And you were the spoilt child dressed in white?

Lena: Yes I suppose so, ha ha ha!

Trevor: Do you remember some of these dresses?

Lena: Oh yes, 'cause somebody said they were all in black and I told them that they weren't in black at all, that dress was brown and hers was navy but m' granny was always in black. It's because the photo is black and white that they thought that I suppose. That was the family as I remembered them and as I told you she had another seven sons, but they were away before I was

there. There were two babies that died at birth and there was a boy who died when he was about 12. He was the first child. Then another uncle died during the First World War.

Trevor: What a size of a family, that's fifteen if I'm counting right! Mind you she doesn't look bad on it does she?

Lena: No, and she'd be in her fifties by the time this photo was taken. She looks amazingly well, but as I remember it she was a great one for delegating the jobs in the house. She had to 'cause she was mother and father to us as she was a widow by this time. I think that her youngest was only three when her husband died. He worked in the granite trade and I remember m' Granny talking about it. He had arthritis and was absolutely helpless before he died. The two of them were arthritic and Cathy was absolutely helpless before she died. Nellie, she just died in 1992, she was 96. I was very close to her, very close.

Trevor: Did you have a happy childhood, from the photographs it looks as though you did?

Lena: Oh yes, I had a happy childhood. I never considered that we were well off but we werna deprived. These girls were working so granny was doing better then.

<u>Top right:</u> Lena in the white dress aged about four. Taken at the back of 88 Bon Accord Street.

<u>Top left:</u> Lena in her Fire Service uniform, which she joined during the Second World War.

<u>Above:</u> In the Fire Service. As you can see, due to shortage of uniforms, most of them only had caps. Lena is in the back row, far left.

The
Backie
Wash Hoose
Sauna

Chapter Five

Mary Johnston

Mary Johnston, a Torry quine born and bred, speaks not only of her memories but also takes a wry look at life in the new millenium. The fascinating photographs portray her folks from the 1850s onwards. George Scroggie, an Aberdonian and a shipyard labourer in the 1860s, begins this group of photographs with Thomas Johnston his son-in-law who came from Yell in the Shetlands. This family bred singular individuals but perhaps more than any other it was James Scroggie, communist and vegetarian, who affirms that ordinary working-class folk of that era often responded to life in a free thinking and individualistic way.

The last few photographs are more loosely connected with the family being the place of work of Thomas Johnston who was Mary's father. However, they encapsulate both an era and an aspect important to Aberdeen - that of the fish preserving industry.

Facing page: Mary as a bridesmaid with a young relative, Patricia McIntosh (niece of the bride) at the wedding of Thomas Lockhart and Lena Robertson.

Mary: These are the earliest photographs I've got of our family. This is my grandmother Jane Muirie Scroggie, born 1857, and this is of my grandfather George Scroggie, who was born about 1851. They were married in 1876. He was a shipyard labourer and docker and my grandmother worked as a papermill worker.

Justine Robertson (Mary's great niece): These dresses, aren't they lovely - were they quite well off at that time or was that their Sunday best?

Mary: They had very little, they married very young. She came down in the world when she married granda. Oh yes. My mother used t' say her grandfather was a writer to the signet but I think that he was just a clerk in a solicitor's office. Her husband was a dock labourer so she married beneath her.

Above left: Jane Muirie Scroggie (nee Findlay). Justine's great, great grandma.

Above right: Justine's great, great grandfather, James Scroggie.

Below: Family group on South Yell, Shetland in the 1930s. Justine's gran is third on the left, back row.

Justine: That's up in Shetland. That's m' gran Jeanie Johnston in the black hat who looked after me when I was young. The Johnston side of the family came from Shetland.

Mary: Yes, that's Yell in Shetland and there's your grandmother and there is the house behind it.

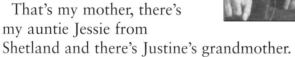

That's my mother, there's my auntie Jessie from Shetland and there's Justine's grandmother.

These are friends of my mother but I don't know who they are, they've got wonderful hats haven't they? Even in my young day we never went out without a hat. I always wore a hat to work all the time until I entered the fish trade in Torry.

Jimmy Scroggie, (1890-1952), lived on cheese and dates. He never married. I don't know what happened to uncle Jimmy, he was antisocial and never visited. Two brothers lived together, Dod and Jimmy.

Justine: And vegetables?

Mary: No vegetables, I don't think he cooked, it was all raw food. My home help is a vegetarian, there's a lot of vegetarians these days. I wouldn't have known what a vegetarian was when I was Justine's age.

Top left: Helen Johnston (nee Scroggie) the daughter of George Scroggie with Justine's grandmother Jane on her lap. Standing, Jessie Peterson, sister to Thomas Johnston. 1911.

Top right: Friends of Helen Johnston wearing their best hats.

Above: A friend of Helen Johnston.

Left: The communist and vegetarian James Scroggie.

Justine: Apart from your uncle.

Mary: But he wasn't classed as a vegetarian - he just ate what he liked, it was just his way of life but none of the rest of the family were like uncle Jimmy. My uncle Dod who lived with him, he was always cooking. They ate separately but Jimmy just had another box o' dates or a lump of cheese!

Trevor: And he became a communist?

Mary: Oh yes, he grew up a communist.

Uncle Willie, he was an iron moulder and worked at Clyne Mitchell which is on South Esplanade West behind Menzies Road. That's uncle Jimmy there he was a dock labourer and so was George. Uncle Findlay, he was a tool maker. We lived in Menzies Road at first 60, then 53.

Justine: Did you go down to Sinclair Road then?

Mary: Oh yes, we were always there. Friday night was cleaning night. There was auntie Jean, auntie Kate, auntie Lizzie who was uncle Willie's wife, my mother and my cousin Madge. So we went down there and cleaned him up on Friday night and then we all sat down and ate a huge apple bannock made by Bendelow's the baker in the Gallowgate.

Trevor: What's this, what is the date?

Mary: You're not publishing that! That's me standing far left. In those days I smiled once a fortnight! I was very serious in those days. That's Torry Intermediate and it didn't open till 1927 and we were the first up, so 1929 is the date of the photograph.

Above: Back - L to R: James Scroggie, George Scroggie
Front - L to R: George Scroggie sen., Alexander Scroggie, Findlay Scroggie

Justine: So these are my great grandmother's brothers then?

Mary: Yes, four boys and granda. That's just the boys though. There was Agnes, there was Helen, there was Jean, there was Cecilia and there was Kate. Five and four's nine but she had fourteen. Granda, Jimmy and Dod all lived at 9 Sinclair Road. Willie and Findlay were both married and the daughters were all married.

Below: Mary at school, standing to the far left back row.

Justine's grandmother and grandfather.

<u>Justine:</u> What did you do after you left school?

<u>Mary:</u> Well I didna stay on, it was all work in these days so I went to James Bisset the booksellers. That was in Mr Bisset's day, long before it was taken over by Blackwells. Mr Milne of the Central Press bought it when Mr Bisset retired, then it was taken over by Blackwells. I went from Bissets into the fish trade when Mr Bisset retired. I went to Hines Brothers in 1945 and I was there till they closed down in 1950, then I went from there to Thomas Wilson's from 1950 to 1981 when I retired. I kept all the books, did the wages and that sort of thing.

<u>Trevor:</u> Did you like the fish better than being at Bisset's?

<u>Mary:</u> No I quite enjoyed being at Bisset's, but it was very old fashioned. The office was a little kiosk about the size of a telephone box with glass all round and there were two of us sitting inside looking out.

Provost Skene's was a lodging house and my mother was friendly with the lodging master's daughter. (Provost Skene's House is now open to the public as a historical house.) The so-called Victorian Room is where the lodging master had his flat. My mother used to go in and play in those rooms. My mother stayed in the Guestrow at that time.

This genetic engineering it's a terrible thing don't you think, what do you think about it? Maybe the younger generation will think it's all right but not anyone of my age would want to condone that. What do you think Justine?

<u>Justine:</u> I think it's according to what it's used for. There could be things that it might be useful for. Do you remember Thalidomide? It might be useful for cases like that.

<u>Mary:</u> Yes, to repair people that would be good but to breed a super-race, we've already had super-races haven't we?

Justine: Hitler was before his time wasn't he?

Mary: If he'd had that he would have been churning them out! Ha ha ha!

Trevor: So what do you think about life today compared to when you were younger, would you rather have lived then than now?

Mary: Life was different altogether and one thing we didn't have, that thing sitting in the corner and we didn't have videos either. We made our own entertainment in those days but it's a big temptation to watch it.

Justine: And you've just got a microwave as well haven't y'?

Mary: You make me sound as though I'd got everything! Ha ha ha! They are a convenience but y' don't do proper cooking with a microwave. I keep my bread in the freezer and when I want to make a bit of toast I take out a slice o' bread and two seconds in the microwave and it's ready for the toaster.

Aberdeen Preserving Company where Justine's great grandfather Thomas Johnston worked. He is seated in the centre. This is the salt fish department, of which he was foreman. 1920s.

My mother had an open fire with a grate and an oven alongside it and the cooking was all done there. There was a gas ring but we'd no cookers. We lived in the same one room which we cooked in. My mother cooked very plain food; it was all stews, soups and milk puddings.

Justine: What did you do for clothes?

Mary: I only had one sister but I had all her hand-me-downs. That was Justine's grandmother. Sometimes my mother was a bit reckless and bought two of each but not very often. Grandma made our dresses, but grandma was the world's worst dress maker and she would make frillows - she loved givin' y' dresses with frills, they were all squint but of course we wore them.

Above: Employees of the Aberdeen Preserving Company, probably from the wet fish department.

Left: Female worker with Clydesdale horse at the Aberdeen Preserving Company.

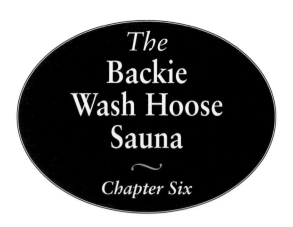

Hilda Youngson

Hilda Youngson's *charming reminiscence allows us a glimpse of a young woman growing up in the west-end where she took the tram down from Queen's Cross to shop, perhaps at Watt and Grant or to visit her father at his work in the Back Wynd where he ran a wholesale saddlers and ironmongers. And where apart from the trams, Hilda says 'It was all horses in those days' furnishing us with a scene quite difficult to imagine nowadays.*

Later we peek at Hilda at work during her apprenticeship in a dispensing chemist where she made pills and dispensed the cure-all Ipecacuanha Wine.

She tells us about the time during the war when she served in the Ambulance Brigade and had to be at the ready in case of an air-raid.

Hilda: This was my grandmother's house at Ardeer, Mannofield, 1917-18. It's a big house with a long avenue. Houses have since been built in the grounds. They went into that house in 1895 and that was my grandfather William Youngson who was a saddler and wholesale ironmonger. They paid £1560 for it and we just loved going up there as children. That's me third from the right in the white hat.

My sister Henzel had her reception at the Palace Hotel after she was married in King's College. That would be in 1937. That's my sister sitting and that's me (fourth on the right) and that's the bridegroom to the left of me.

Above: Hilda's grandparent's home at Mannofield. Hilda is third from the right, front row.

Below: Hilda's sister Henzel's wedding reception. Hilda is fourth from the right.

My mother and father were also married at the Palace Hotel, which was burned down during the war.

Trevor: Which school did you go to when you were a child?

Hilda: Broomhill. At that time mum and dad lived in Hammerfield Avenue so that's where I went. Ardeer was quite close so it was convenient for us to run up there and see our grandmother. It was a lovely time for us as children going up there. We then moved to Carlton Place and then I went to Mile End School.

Above: Hilda's mother and father on their honeymoon. They look as if they were climbing, very difficult for the ladies with their long skirts. The photograph was taken in Switzerland, possibly Mount Pelatus.

Below: Mile End School - Hilda top left aged about 10. The headmaster was called Mr Sutherland.

Trevor: What did you do when you left school?

Hilda: I had a four year apprenticeship in dispensing and I was dispensing mostly all the time after that. I served my apprenticeship in Torry and then I went to Midstocket Road, later I worked in the hospital for a while and afterwards I was in Fountainhall Road.

Trevor: What are you doing in this photograph at Mile End School?

Hilda Youngson, second from the left. The photo was taken at Mile End School in the 1940s.

Hilda: Well, during the Second World War we were attached to the Ambulance Brigade, that was Dr Florence Stephen who was head of us and we had to take nights; some of us had to go on even dates and others went on odd dates. We had to take duties in Mile End School all night also.

Trevor: What did you actually do?

Hilda: Well I suppose we didn't do that much unless there was an air raid on. However, we were never called out but if we had been we would have done all the first aid.

Trevor: What did your father do before the war?

Hilda: He and my uncle Sam had a business in Back Wynd opposite the cemetery. It was a wholesale saddlers and ironmongers and his father ran it before him. It was he who owned Ardeer. The name of the company was George Littlejohn. I don't know who the Littlejohns were but it must have been there a long time. We used to go there quite often to see our father, my grandfather was also there, right at the top. Henzel also worked there for a wee while.

Joyce: (Hilda's niece) Did she? That's Henzel whose wedding photograph you've got there?

Hilda: Yes, she went there and worked in the office, typing I think but I'm not quite sure. She soon got fed up with that and went in for her music.

My father carried on in the business for a long while but he was not well so I think they sold it because of that, and not because the demand for saddles had dropped. Shirras Laing had it and now it's something else.

Joyce: Y' know when you go down the Back Wynd there's an archway through which there were other buildings; that was where it was. It's now a cafe called Littlejohns curiously enough. Being in saddles, did your dad ever ride a horse?

Hilda: Well, during the First World War he was a signaller. There are some photographs of him in uniform and I think he had something to do with horses there.

Although not on horseback, the jodhpurs distinguish the central pair as horsemen.
Hilda's father is on the right whilst 'Finnie' Reid, Hilda's uncle is far right.

When the horses went out of use and the demand for saddles fell it made a huge difference to the business. It was all horses before then.

Trevor: What did you do after finishing dispensing?

Hilda: I just came home to look after my mum for a while. I think I gave up work before I retired so that I could look after mum. I worked for Anderson and Spence for many years, that was in Fountainhall Road.

The interior of Davidson and Kay's chemist shop.
219 Union Street, 1950s.

Joyce: It's a really lovely chemist, it's one of the few chemists where they have still got the original display cabinet and counter.

Hilda: Yes, I'm glad that some of these old things were kept. I think that they still have some of the old carboys but I don't know if they still have them in the window. It was just coloured water that they kept in them and we sometimes had to fill them up when I worked for a previous pharmacy.

When a prescription came in I had to make up the mixtures, etcetera pills or cachets which were made out of rice paper. We didn't have to make the tablets but we had to make the pills. We had to weigh up all the ingredients first, then mix with a pestle and mortar, then we had to roll them out and they had to be exactly even. They were then put on a pill-cutting machine, cut them into little bits which we then rolled into the pills and then varnished.

Joyce: What did you put into the cachets?

Hilda: We had to make up all the powders first, divide them up, weigh them and put them into the cachets. What a job!

Trevor: Didn't you like it then?

Hilda: I liked it well enough but when you look back what a lot of work it involved. Besides the pills and cachets there were a lot of mixtures that you had to make up.

Trevor: Were there medicines that a lot of people took?

Hilda: Black Draught was a great favourite. I used to have to make up this stock which consisted of mostly senna, liquorice and gardamm. I forget all of the ingredients now but it was a laxative mainly. That was when I was in Torry, it was a sort of cure all. Yes they seemed t' like the Black Draught but it must have been dreadful stuff to take!

Trevor: It was Friars Balsam when I was a child in the 1940s.

Hilda: Oh yes, Friars Balsam that was a great thing for steaming wasn't it. I remember also the doctor coming and giving us castor oil then giving us a caramel afterwards to take away the taste, it was awful stuff to take. Another frequently used cure was Ipecacuanha Wine & Chlorodyne.

Trevor: What's that?

Hilda: Ha ha ha! It was made to help bring up phlegm. I don't think we had to make that, it was just a tincture. I had to make the Chlorodyne, however.

Trevor: Tell us something about what you did for holidays when you were a child.

Hilda: When we were away we didn't go further than Torphins or Banchory, we didn't go abroad at that time.

Dad had an old car and he would take us to Torphins for our month's holidays. I think we occupied the whole house where we stayed but the people who owned it used t' cook for us. They probably just occupied one room. In one house we stayed, we used to have to go through the kitchen, so mother asked them if they could make a door so that we didn't have to go through their living quarters. We mainly went walks and played tennis or went cycling, just simple things. Dad used to come out on the train to see us. He'd a bicycle that he left at the station.

Dad would take me down to Watt & Grant's and buy me a lovely coat with a cape. That was when we were in

**Hilda's family leaving Torphins
in their father's motor car.**

Carlton Place but what we did when we were younger was a different matter. You could get what they called a sight of clothes from Watt and Grant in a big box. You could try them on and if they didn't fit you could send them back. That would be in the 1920s and 30s. I think it's where the McDonalds is now in Union Street.

Joyce: Besides Watt & Grant there was Frasers, that was Falconers originally, and Reid & Pearson in George Street and of course Esslemont & MacIntosh.

Hilda: There were lovely shops in Union Street in those days. We used to get the tram down, there was a circular Queens Cross which used t' go right round. It started at the Castlegate and went up Rosemount or it went the other way.

We sometimes went bathing and the bathers would change themselves in those little huts, it was very discreet. Horses were there and when the tide went out the horses were there to pull them out or vice-versa. Although we used one of these bathing huts we didn't really swim, it was more paddling that we did because it wasn't till we went to school that we got swimming lessons.

Hilda with Henzel (left) and a four footed friend, aged mid 20s with the Pentland Firth in the background.

The
Backie
Wash Hoose
Sauna
~
Chapter Seven

Alan Findlay

Alan Findlay's photographs trace a period mainly before he was born and begins with his great grandmother. Not much is known about her and it is mostly because she is photographically the oldest of the dynasty that she begins this group of photographs. The central person is Alan Findlay's father, John, who is first seen in his Gordon Highlander's uniform. He was subsequently wounded twice in the trenches before training as a barber and practising his trade in the Spital in Old Aberdeen. Later he took on another shop in the city centre.

He then worked as a taxi driver with Campbell's Taxis and later at Culter Paper Mill until he retired at 65.

Alan Findlay, a long serving employee of the Culter Paper Mills, now works at the Stoneywood Paper Mills.

<u>Above:</u> This is a family picnic at Balmedie in the 1920s. Alan's father is back left, his grandfather is in front of him and his grandmother to his left.

<u>Facing page:</u> Alan sitting on the doorstep of 6 Craigton Crescent, Culter. A late comer to the family there were 15 years difference between him and the previous sibling.

Taken at Park Hill where she lived, this is the old granny who was my mother's grandmother. Cruickshank was her family name. She is perhaps the oldest member of my family that I have a photo of.

The picture below, that's the 7th Gordons at Culter being mobilised for war in August 1914. My father is there somewhere but it's difficult to see.

My father is in the centre with a chum's arm across his chest. He was about 16 or 17 years old and the picture would have been taken at the beginning of the First World War. This was the 7th Gordons around the remains of a camp fire. With empty frying pans, billycans and shovels they must have finished their meal and were taking their tea. Where the photo was taken I don't know but the photographer, Scot and Co. was based in Kirkcaldy.

My father was wounded twice
in the First World War. Here you
can see him with a wounded arm
sitting next to the nurse at the front. I
think the photo was taken in Woodend.

This is my father with his brother Alexander. He was a milkman for
the Co-op I think. As you can see my father's barber shop was on the
boundary of the Spital and College Bounds.

My father, on the right poised with a cut throat razor in his barber
shop at 193 the Spital.

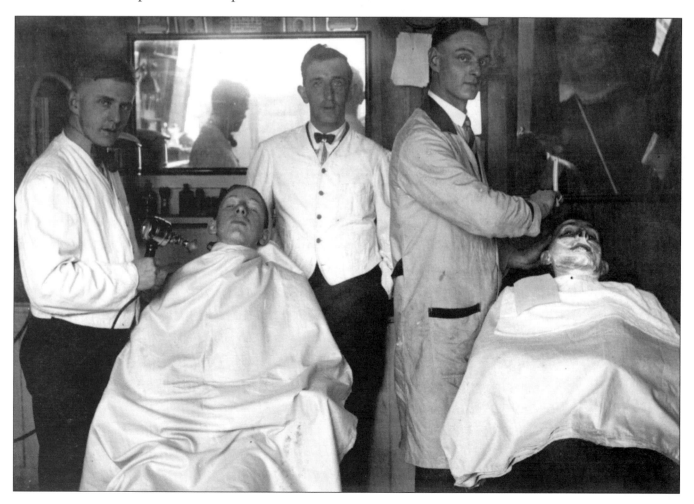

This is uncle Sandy and his milk cart again. Those solid wheels and those cassies would have made for a bumpy, noisy hurl.

Family photo at Jamaica Street. That's my grandfather on the left wearing the trilby, standing behind my father. My granny is at the back beside my mother. I was a bit scared of them because they were Victorian and were quite strict and he wouldna' stand any nonsense. I didn't see that much of them because they lived in Aberdeen and I lived in Culter.

This is my mother's family, she is sitting third from the left behind the child. My grandmother and grandfather are at the opposite sides of the photo. The three young men at the back went to Canada as so many did in those days.

The family used to rent a farm out at Peterculter called Ordhill and they used to go for their school holidays. This was before I was born as were most of these photos. I went there with my family and my uncle Sandy's family. Uncle Sandy was the one who was a milkman. My older brother would make the carties but we would have to leave them behind to the kids in Culter when the holiday finished.

My father took a cataract in his eye and at that time they were experimenting with radium. They used it to try and treat the cataract but they burned his eye and ruined it and he ended up with a plastic eye. Eventually they fitted a plastic eye to the muscles of the eye so that it moved and looked more natural. He had years and years of agony with that and he eventually ended up with a brain tumour that was possibly caused by that radium treatment.

This was taken by a street photographer and here's me on the right with one of my chums on Union Bridge. Somethings don't seem to change much, what with the leopards and Jamieson & Carry, it's exactly the same today. That would have been in the 50s and I'd still have been at school.

Alan Findlay's father, a keen bowling enthusiast, mows the green at the Culter Bowling Club, 1950s.

Alan with his parents at Balmoral, 1950s.

Persley Bridge. I don't know where this photo came from, we just had it in the family but I think my grandfather on my mother's side had it. The bridge looks quite new so perhaps it was taken about the time it was finished.

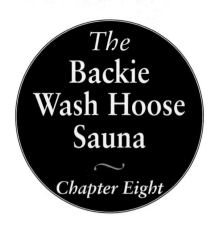

William McHardy

William McHardy is one of those people lucky enough to have largely completed his family tree within recent history. It traces the line of his father's family through a rural life in the Durris area. However, as in most of these memoirs, emigration often looms large.

Emigration had occurred even before the Clearances and had thus already paved a way for a later generation whose conditions were more than often hard, and where the enticements of free land away from 'ungenerous landlords' were attractive enough for some family members to emigrate lock, stock and barrel.

William, however, coming from a later era which allowed working folk, through education, to realise their own potential, stayed here in Aberdeenshire, still with the land but in the capacity of a soil scientist.

Trevor: How did you come to go to the Macaulay Institute?

William McHardy: Well I was fairly bright at school and it was easy to get into university in those days if you'd got the right number of highers. I went to university in Aberdeen where I did my first degree in chemistry then I did a Phd. also in chemistry. In those days, in terms of getting a job there was a choice of where you could go. ICI, Distillers and Shell to name but a few, all came round on recruiting drives. Most people could count on two or three job offers and I think the record among my contemporaries was 10!

Trevor: What date was that?

William: It was in 1961. It was one of my friends who pointed out that there was a job going at the Macaulay Institute for Soil Research. They were looking for what they called an experimental pedologist. I was not at all sure what this was but the qualifications were a degree and post graduate experience in either chemistry or geology. I applied with four others and I was lucky enough to get the job. The main reason for taking it, I think, was that I could stay in this part of the world. With most other jobs it would have meant going south, so I thought that this was a chance to stay at home and so it came to be that I spent my whole working career at the Macaulay Institute.

Trevor: What is a pedologist ?

William: Pedology is a scientific term for soil science really. The impression at my interview was that my role was going to be to set up artificial columns of soil, putting in solutions at the top and seeing what came out of the bottom or what changes in mineralogy within the artificial soil column would occur. However, when I started I was set to building an apparatus to measure the surface areas of fine powders of soil, or soil clays if you like, by gas absorption. So I got into physical chemistry with soil clays as the raw material. I messed about with that for a year or two until they bought an electron microscope, with which it was possible to look directly at fine clay particles which were beyond the resolution of a conventional light microscope. In 1965 I took over from the original electron microscopist and remained more or less in this capacity for the rest of my career. I provided a service for other projects within the research programme that wanted to use electron microscopy. Latterly we sold our services to the oil companies and the commercial world in general.

Trevor: Was the electron microscope a big breakthrough at that time?

William: Yes, as the Director at the time commented, it had great visitor value. In other words it was quite a spectacular piece of high tech equipment to show off with. It had been invented just before the war and then came into commercial production in about the 50s. We got one quite early on, one of the first in Aberdeen I think but like all these things when I look back, what was achieved with it was probably some way short of early expectations.

Trevor: Where were you born and brought up?

William: I was born in Durris on the south side of the Dee some 12 miles from Aberdeen and I now live six miles from where I was born.

This is a photograph of my great-grandfather, John McHardy, his first wife, Robina Jamieson and their first child, Caroline.

Caroline was born in February 1867 so this picture must date from later that year. John was keeper at Morven Lodge, Glengairn and latterly in the employ of the Keiller family (the Dundee jam makers), from about 1880 until his death in 1904. Robina died at Morven Lodge in 1885 having borne 10 children. John married again in 1887, to the servant of the Glengairn priest. She had one child before dying shortly afterwards. His third wife, whom he married in 1894 bore him another six children, the last of whom was born several months after his own death.

Head gamekeepers in those days must have had a bit of status and influence because his funeral rated a short write-up in the Aberdeen Daily Journal, in which it was recorded that in attendance, among other notable citizens was Provost Walker. I got this photograph from Beth McHardy who lives in Fraserburgh and is one of John McHardy's last surviving granddaughters from his first family. She recalls seeing a newspaper cutting in which the presence of nobility at John's funeral was reported but I have been unable to find this so far.

This is the wedding of Caroline McHardy (the child in the photograph on p77) to Valentine Macdonald which took place on the 13th of January 1891 at St. Mary's Roman Catholic Church in Huntly Street. Seated left is John McHardy, the bride's father and seated right is Mary McHardy the bride's sister. Standing on the extreme left is my grandfather, Alexander and next to him his elder brother, Charles. The photograph was taken by 'Craigen' of 17 Crown Street, Aberdeen.

Trevor: Do you remember any of them ?

William: No, I don't remember any of these people. My grandfather died in 1913 aged 42. He was Catholic but my grandmother wasn't and with his death, contact with his siblings seems to have been lost. It is only recently that I have managed to get in touch with one or two of their descendents. For example a copy of this wedding photograph was sent to me by Caroline Tanner who lives in British Columbia. She is a granddaughter of Valentine Macdonald and, like me, a great-grandchild of John McHardy.

Valentine Macdonald was a prison warder at Peterhead at the time of his marriage. Later, he carried on a licensed business at Aberdeen and Banchory. He was also a heavy athlete. Big Mac, as he was called, was described in his obituary in 1924 as having been one of the tallest athletes in Scotland being 6ft 5ins in height, weighing over 23 stones and with a chest measurement of 52 inches. He would train by walking out to Blairs to attend Mass, often in full highland dress. He was a devout Catholic noted for his generosity toward Catholic causes.

My aunt Ruby remembered visits from the Macdonald family to Spyhill Cottage in Durris. They would arrive by horse and carriage for Sunday lunch. Big Mac's size left a lasting impression on her. Occasionally, on their visits he would be accompanied by his great friend and fellow athlete A.A. Cameron. Ruby remembered him as being even bigger than Big Mac. A.A. Cameron was the top heavy athlete of his day and had something of an international reputation.

This is another of Beth McHardy's photographs which she described as a picnic at Craigendarroch. The central couple are James and Mary Grant (nee McHardy) with their first child, Caroline (Carrie) seated on James's knee. Mary was the bridesmaid in the Valentine Macdonald wedding group. Carrie was born on the 3rd of June 1896 which means that this photograph dates from about 1897. The bowler-hatted gentleman, middle left seated on a low stool is William Aeneas Grant 1872-1952, a brother of

James and grandfather of Sheila Grant, a former working colleague of mine whom I have to thank for providing me with much of the information about this photograph. William Grant was on course to become a priest but he discovered that he didn't have the vocation and joined the police instead. He became superintendent of the Dumbartonshire Police. In the top left hand corner is Charles Joseph Grant, the youngest brother who died in 1901. Next to him wearing a glengarry is my great grandfather, John McHardy, and second from the right on the back row wearing a bonnet, is my grandfather Alexander McHardy. James and Mary Grant emigrated to Saskatoon in 1904 by which time they had four children. James's younger sister Marjory accompanied them. She is also in this photograph seated in front of Mary. She married William Pike in Canada and had three sons.

Trevor: What are the details of their emigration?

William: The family had occupied the farm of Abergairn, two miles west of Ballater, for several generations. James Grant's father, also James, had been factor to the then owner of the Morven Estate, the Marquis of Huntly, by whom he was gifted a small parcel of land on which he was allowed to build the family home. When he asked for deeds to prove ownership the old Marquis had replied in words to the effect that they were both 'gentlemen' and that there was no need for a piece of paper between them. However the son or possibly the grandson of the Marquis fell on hard times - it is thought he was a gambler who lost heavily and ultimately had to sell the estate. The purchaser of the Morven estate was John Keillor of Dundee who refused to honour the transaction between the Grants and the old Marquis. Apparently the Keillers were unpopular landlords and withdrew many privileges, such as access for the locals to use paths on the estate to visit the manse and kirk. In one incident the minister was thrown off their frozen pond where he was skating.

Thus the locals had a joint grievance against the ruined Marquis for causing the sale and the Keillers for being ungenerous landlords. Possibly James Grant's rent would have been increased to cover the house that he in reality owned as well as the farm tenancy and it is reasonable to suppose that this injustice, together with the fact that the Canadian Government were offering 200 acres of land in an attractive package to potential settlers, would have influenced their decision to emigrate.

I have a couple of articles which were sent to me from Canada in which Carrie described what life was like in the early pioneering days in Saskatoon. Carrie visited this country in the early 1980s when she was in her 80s. Unfortunately at this time I was completely unaware of her existence. I have only discovered about all of this since I retired. She died in Vancouver in 1986 at the age of 90.

That's my grandfather, Alexander McHardy, my granny and their family. The boy at the centre back is James the eldest, who became a police inspector with the Manchester Police. Far left is Robina, she must have been called after her granny. She started off in service and ended up as cook / housekeeper at Scone Palace. She used to say that when she started, a cook in a big house had status because there were lots of staff to do all the chores. By the time she reached the top she had to do everything herself, even walk the dog. She died in 1994 aged 92.

Trevor: Your grandfather, what did he do?

William: Like his father, he was a gamekeeper. The photo was taken in about 1910 at Spyhill Cottage which still stands. It's midway between Stonehaven and Banchory on the Slug Road. That's my father, William in the middle behind the dog. That's Alick in his sailor suit and Maggie at the end. Alick was killed in the Second World War and Maggie died as a result of a burning accident in 1928. While in service to a minister in Aberdeen she was ironing one day with a gas iron whilst the minister's wife was using a bowl of petrol to

clean a felt hat. The iron came too close to the petrol which then caught fire. Maggie made the classic mistake of lifting up the bowl to put it outside. The flames blew back on her and she was so severely burned that she died in hospital the next day. It was a terrible tragedy for the family.

These are the children of the family at the door of the cottage, my father is on the right leaning nonchalantly against the door post. They seem to be wearing the same clothes as in the photograph above so it must have been taken about the same time.

My father, again on the right, with the rest of the children taken a year or so later. Sailor suits were still in fashion though. This is a professional photograph by Messers Prophet of Dundee. Taken at Spyhill Cottage with the Slug Road in the background. Photographers must have been plying their trade by going door to door.

Trevor: Do you think that you would have been considered reasonably well off?

William: I think as a gamekeeper's family they would have been quite comfortable. My grandfather would have been in quite a good position for bringing home something for the pot. He had a good relationship with the neighbouring farmer, where he helped out with a bit of casual labour in exchange for farm produce and the use of a pony and trap when for example visitors had to be met at Crathes

Station. When my grandfather died in 1913, the day after Charlie his sixth child was born, things must have become very difficult. However the laird was quite paternalistic and didn't like to see the family of a good member of his staff become homeless and destitute through no fault of their own, so he gave them a house, rent free, at the Kirkton of Durris which had a laundry attached. It had been built for a man and his two daughters who had upped and gone to Canada. So my grandmother took in washing to make ends meet. I remember my father talking of how he and Alick, before going to school, would have to push a barrow-load of laundry along to Park Crossroads on the South Deeside Road to meet a carrier. This was a round trip of four miles whilst school was then a round trip of another four miles - in the opposite direction! I don't think that the laundry trip would have been every day but it would have probably been at least once a week. This would have been at the time of the First World War and with the proliferation of establishments for housing wounded soldiers there would have been no shortage of dirty washing. I know my father was allowed to leave school early, before the age of 14, so that he could start bringing in some money. Another indication of their impoverished circumstances was Charlie's first pair of working breeks. These had been made by my granny from a discarded pair of his oldest brother's police trousers. This was fine except the truncheon pocket made their origin fairly obvious and led to a good deal of ribbing from his workmates.

When my father won the King's Cup at the Aberdeen Wapinschaw in 1926 he was described as having been a gardener for three years. However in my birth certificate of 1936 his occupation is given as estate forester. I know he left the estate for a period and worked for the Forestry Commission, which unfortunately disqualified him from benefiting from the laird's will, which he would have done had his service been unbroken.

After the war my father became assistant gardener at Durris House and when the head gardener left in 1948 he got the job, although the post of assistant was never filled. We moved into the gardener's cottage, which was a big improvement in our accommodation because it had a flush toilet and a backboiler. There was no bathroom or electricity however. For baths - not taken everyday - a portable bath in the washhouse was used. Eventually after much lobbying one of the bedrooms was converted into a proper bathroom. Bathing became more frequent. My father's next step was to try and persuade the factor to put in electricity. We were told that to bring the mains electricity to our house would be exorbitantly expensive but we could install a generator supply at our own expense. My father did not take kindly to this idea and got to hear (from the kirk beadle) of a gardener/handyman job going in Milltimber with a modern house complete with bathroom and electricity. His prospective employer was Godfrey P Geddes of Culter Paper Mill. Lt. Col. Geddes had been commanding officer of the 5/7 battalion of the Gordon Highlanders before the war. This was my father's battalion so I think the interview went very well and in November 1961 we moved to Milltimber. When Col. Geddes died my father carried on looking after the widow, doing the garden and chauffeuring.

That's my mother and father with my sister and myself when I was nine and my sister was three. The photo was taken in June 1945 just before my father was demobbed. In the background is Durris House which was requisitioned during the war for troops to live in.

In the last months (or possibly just weeks) of my father being in the army he was stationed in Banchory and was issued with a motorbike with which he could commute from home. My mother would say later that this was the only time during the war that she worried about his safety. (Two of her brothers had been killed in separate motorcycle accidents before the war.) My father's own sticky moment during this final period was being sent on his motorbike to investigate a suspected mine washed up on the shore at Catterline or some such place. Very much to his relief the 'mine' proved to be nothing more than an empty oil drum.

This picture appeared in the Press and Journal of Saturday the 7th of August 1926. It is of my father being presented with the King's Cup which was the top prize at the Aberdeen Wapinschaw which was held at the Black Dog rifle ranges and organised by the Aberdeen, Aberdeenshire and Kincardineshire Territorial Rifle Association. My father was only 20 at the time of his success but he had already been a 'Terrier' for three years. My father and later his brothers competed most years until the outbreak of war in 1939, and were usually in the prize money. For example in 1933 Charlie came home with 15 shillings, my father 10 shillings (a poor year for him) and Alick got 10 shillings for coming third in the Recruits Cup.

In the 1920s and 30s the Wapinschaw merited quite comprehensive reporting by the Press and Journal, even down to what was said in the speeches at the prize-giving. In the year of my father's triumph the targets of the two leading marksmen were published, indicating how my father and his nearest challenger, a Lieut. G. Scott, in the final stage placed their 15 shots at 600 yards.

After celebrating his King's Cup victory my father was on his way home with two of his pals on a motor bike and side-car. At one point they ran off the road and capsized in a field. No one was hurt and the machine was got back on to its wheels and off they set again oblivious to the fact that their rifles were no longer in the side-car but were being dragged along the road behind them, no doubt in a shower of sparks. Damage to the rifles, the property of the Territorial Army, was considerable and could not be covered up. My father reckoned that they were lucky to escape from being in serious trouble. It is possible that if he hadn't just won the King's Cup, thus bringing glory and prestige to the local battalion, they would have been thrown out of the Territorials altogether.

This group was taken at a civilian 'shoot' at the Loch of Leyes near Crathes sometime in the 30s. It may have been a press photograph. Charlie is standing in the back row 3rd from left and Alick 7th from left. My father is kneeling in the middle row 2nd from left. Seated directly in front of him is his great pal, Ken Shepherd - another frequent prize winner at the Wapinschaw. My father and his brothers were not universally welcomed at these meetings. Alick once overheard a competitor complain, "They bloody McHardys are here again. Naebody else'll hae a chance!"

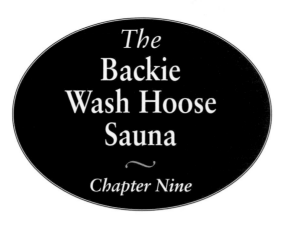

The Backie Wash Hoose Sauna

~ Chapter Nine

Ted Munro

*T*ed's grandfather was "washed out of a salmon
cobble and drowned." This event did not seem
to affect Ted's choice of trade as he became a
trawl fisherman in the 1920s. However, he observes
that the conditions on board a trawler were intolerable
and that fishermen often lived worse than animals, he
avers that there was never a time in which he felt in
danger during storms and high seas. Although Ted is
known mostly for his reminiscences about his life as a
fisherman, here he also gives us some interesting details
of his life on dry land.

Above: Ted (second left) with some of his school pals.

Facing page: Ted on board the 'Fernbank' (built 1910).
This would be around 1935.

Ted Munro: This is a receipt for a Singer sewing machine, price seven pounds and was bought by my mother Jemima Munro in 1918. The address on it is St. Peter's Place which is in the Spital, in fact it's the back gate to the St Peter's Cemetery in King Street. It was a house in the Spital next to the Red Lion Pub. It had a basement which had two rooms. In those days you could pretty well choose a house to live in because there were plenty o' empty houses then.

their work as they both worked in the comb industry. The professions of the fathers are interesting - a mason's labourer and a marine stoker. Granite and fishing y' can't get more Aberdonian than that.

Ted: The man who owned the combworks in Hutcheon Street started a combworks in Toronto but he didn't have any experienced workers to run the factory. So he asked a lot of the workers here if they would like to go out to Canada. My father

No.	When, Where, and How Married.	Signatures of Parties. Rank or Profession, whether Single or Widowed, and Relationship (if any).	Age.	Usual Residence.	Name, Surname, and Rank or Profession of Father. Name, and Maiden Surname of Mother.	If a regular Marriage, Signatures of officiating Minister and Witnesses. If irregular Date of Conviction, Decree of Declarator, or Sheriff's Warrant.	When and Where Registered, and Signature of Registrar.
196	On the twentyninth day of November. At Trades Hall, Belmont Street, Aberdeen. After publication according to the forms of the Congregational Church.	(Signed) James Munro, Combmaker, (Bachelor). (Signed) Jemima Mennie, Combworker, (Spinster).	20. 20.	19, Guestrow, Aberdeen. 66, Virginia Street, Aberdeen.	Hugh Munro, Masons labourer, Matilda Munro, ms. Dickie James Mennie, Marine stoker (dec) Ann Aldridge, previously Mennie ms. Hay.	(Signed) R. McGairney, Congregational Church. (Signed) Robina Cumming, Witness. David McDonald, Witness.	1907 December Second At Aberdeen. (Signed) James G. Craib Registrar.

1907

This is the marriage certificate of my mother and father. The marriage of James Munro and Jemima Mennie in 1907. He was living at 19 Guestrow and she at 66 Virginia Street.

Trevor: They must have got together at

volunteered and off he went. Unfortunately he didn't like it but couldn't afford to get back. His fare out to Canada was paid but not back, so he had to save up for two or three years before he could afford to get back and I think he came back in a cattle boat. He came back in about 1914 and that's as far back as I can remember. They were living in a house in Cotton Street. I was born about four years before he went away.

Trevor: So you were born in 1910?

Ted: Yes, that's right. He left m' mother, myself and a cousin that my mother brought up. If he'd have got on as well as his brothers had he'd a been alright. After Cotton Street we moved down to Fittie.

No.	Name and Surname.	When and Where Born.	Sex.	Name, Surname, and Rank or Profession of Father. Name, and Maiden Surname of Mother. Date and Place of Marriage.	Signature and Qualification of Informant, and Residence, if out of the House in which the Birth occurred.	When and Where Registered, and Signature of Registrar.
7	Jemima Mennie	1887 March Thirteenth 7h. 0m. P.M 10 Village of Findon Portlethen	F	James Mennie Salmon fisher Ann Mennie M.S. Hay 1881 January 1st Aberdeen	(Signed) James Mennie Father (Present)	1887 March 22nd At Portlethen (Signed) Charles Meston Registrar.

Extracted from the Register Book of Births, for the District of Portlethen, in the County of Kincardine, this 22nd day of March 1887. Charles Meston, Registrar.

Trevor: So this is your mother's birth certificate. 13th of March 1887.

Ted: She was born at number 10 Findon, there were no streets just a number on the houses. I went to find the house but I could never find it. I since learned that it had been knocked down. My grandfather was a salmon fisher in Findon and was washed out of his salmon fisher's cobble and drowned. He would have caught the fish and my grandmother smoked them but when he was lost she couldna stay in Portlethen so they come into Aberdeen and they got the house in 66 Virginia Street.

Trevor: How old was he when he was drowned?

Ted: He was 29. There were two of them; being fisher people they had bye names because many of them had the same name and he was called a 'Bar'

These two pictures show the salmon fishers on the River Dee at the turn of the century. The building in the top picture is still used by fishermen to this day.

and the other brother wis a 'Clipper'. The 'Clipper' lived to a ripe old age. I don't know what 'Bar' meant but a 'Clipper' was a long pole with a hook on the end of it. If you had a big fish you put the hook in the head o' it to pull it on to the ship.

That's the wife's brother (above right) and I hadna seen him for years. I was at a camp called Sidibish which is near Alexandria and he was at another camp called Siddigaber(?) I was there for about six weeks and he'd been there for about 18 months. I was walking down the street in Alexandria and I met him. Previously I hadn't seen him for about 12 years!

Trevor: Being a fisherman did your wife stay at home?

Ted: We got married on the 27th of December 1935. We only did about 10 trips in a year if we were lucky. Durin' the summer we went from the Pentland Firth to Dinnet Head. Then y' set y' course for the Westerman Isle. To get there we went up the north-east coast of Iceland and there's a big fiord up there. At the entrance to it was a big herrin' centre where we got our

bait. Up by the north cape past the ice barrier, then off Iceland maybe 150 mile so you were half way across t' Greenland, and you worked there till you had enough fish to come hame. Then y' set your course fae there and apart from perhaps a glimpse o' the Westerman Isle the next land that you saw was Dinnet Head. So after being married on the 27th December, I was away on the 9th o' January. We went for bait and we lay there afore we got herrin' to bait the lines. We come home and we had a 25 day

Above: Ted and his wife on their wedding day.

Left: Ted on the 'Fernbank'. He spent about 5 years on this vessel.

Below: Panoramic view of Aberdeen harbour. c 1940s

settlin' which meant that it was 25 days that you were away. I gave the wife £9, that was a fortune at that time.

However, that was going to have to last another 25 days. She was brought up with the Gordon Highlanders. She was born in the Castle Hill and her father, who had signed up in 1908, travelled with the regiment. They had married quarters there and it was only when the regiment was going to go from Aldershot to Gibraltar, which meant a longer contract, that he packed it in in 1935. That was 26 years he was in the Gordons.

Above: On the *'Struan'* - gutting fish.

Below: L-R Ted's father, mother and sister Ina with three cousins sitting on a salmon cobble.

My wife, when she was 14 was put home to her grandmother where she was brought up till she was married.

Because conditions were so bad I packed up the trawlin' and we went t' Glasgow to try and find work, but we didna give up the house in Aberdeen. When I went to the Labour Exchange in Glasgow and the man said, "Trawl fisherman, you'll never get a job doon here." An' I said, "That's why I cam doon here!" There was a galvanising place and I got a job in there.

Trevor: You'd have enjoyed that!

Ted: Well, after bein' in the open air at sea, I was workin' on the top

Top: This train was called *'Bon Accord'* and ran from the harbour to the gas works on Miller Street (shown here) every 20 minutes from midnight throughout the night. Ted lived to the left of the picture in Baltic Place. Between the houses was Yeats Lane where many sea Captains lived.

Above: Crew and some local youngsters on board the trawler *'Ben Cairn'* in Allisund, Norway, 1927.

of 80 tons o' molten galvanising metal. Toilet cisterns was one thing we did and you'd put in maybe 20 or 30 and you'd t' fish them up wi a long rod with a hook on the end. One day the manager he come inta the canteen and he sez, "As from the end of the week you'll all be reserved at the age of 21. Then we got in five Rangers football players so they would have a reserved occupation. I put in my notice and he said, "Y' don't mean t' say that y' goin' t' leave and go to war?" I said, "I'll tell y' this much, even if the war lasts two or three years I'm goin' t' see the finish o' it, but nae here." I'd turned like a Chinaman! The fumes were turning me yellow! Well I got right back to Aberdeen after bein' there barely a year. I got back on the Sunday, went down t' the fish market on the Monday mornin' and I was away t' sea Monday afterneen.

Left: Unloading fish at Aberdeen Fish Market, 1920s. This was around the time Ted started trawling.

Below: Aberdeen harbour around the time Ted was born.

Trevor: How old were you when you first went to sea?

Ted: I was nine year old. The first time I spent overnight aboard a trawler was when we left Aberdeen on the Friday and down to St David's on the Friday night loaded the coal during the night. We left St. David's at four in the mornin' and back t' Aberdeen for Saturday forenoon. I was nine years old then and that was the beginning of my fishing career. Y' didna get a bed. In the cabin where y' ate your food there wis a place which was the stern o' the ship, and I slept there. I jist did little jobs like.

Margaret McKay

Whilst sailing up the Caledonian Canal (as a child) Margaret McKay overheard that the first shots of the First World War had been fired. At this time in 1914 she was five years old. The clarity of this reminiscence and those that follow indicate that what is said about long term memory is true in that its lucidity grows keener as time moves on.

After spending 50 years in Aberdeen she moved north to live in Morayshire where she lives to this day. As a westender she furnishes us with the detail of life in that area. Its streets and shops are described in loving detail. She attended The Aberdeen High School for Girls situated in Albyn Place where began her great interest in drama, which later often culminated in performances at His Majesty's Theatre.

Above: Margaret aged about two.

Facing page: Margaret with two 'friends' sitting outside a cottage.

I was asked recently what Aberdeen was like before the oil. Well, since it was my hometown from my birth in 1909 till I left it in 1961, here are some memories of the earliest times.

I think it was a good beginning for an Aberdonian that my mother was brought up in the country and my father in town, since the link between town and country there was always so strong.

Aberdeen used to be advertised as 'The Silver City by the Sea.' Remembering churches with tall spires, the front of Marischal College, well-planned terraces, fine town houses, shops and tenements built alike in strong grey granite, and the foghorn booming over all on a misty night reminding of the sea - the description was not too fantastic in those days.

The house where we lived was like so many more spreading over private estates. The whole house had two flats. Downstairs there were four main rooms whilst upstairs had an extra storey. Heating was by coal fires with a big kitchen range, later changing to a gas cooker and gas fires in bedrooms.

Before the First World War this was still an area where visiting cards were exchanged with 'At Home' days stating when the lady of the house could expect visitors to be entertained for afternoon tea.

Where did we shop? In fact we were very well served in Whitehall Road. There was a handy little grocery shop where it was joined by Hamilton Place Lane, and farther up the Lane at Mile End there were more grocers, a chemist, newsagent, a

Above: How to get about in the 1900s. Morayshire.

draper, a plumber and bakers who sent message-boys on bikes to deliver delicious freshly baked Aberdeen butteries for breakfast. These are not to be associated with the flat indigestible lumps of dough often sold under the name today, which bring no credit to the city! Back to the shops. At the foot of Whitehall Road joining Desswood Place, there was another chemist, newsagent, grocer and a dairy with a stable at the back for the horses from Mastrick Farm, who took the milk to our houses. There were plenty of shops within walking distance but the dominant one all over town was 'The Northern Co-operative Society' - the 'Co-op'. Our nearest Co-op was in Midstocket Road opposite Beechgrove Church, where they had a butcher, grocer and baker. Orders were delivered to our doors by horse and cart.

I clearly remember the beginning of the First World War. With my parents I had been visiting a colleague of my father at Kinlochleven where the great new interest was in the huge new pipeline. We left from Ballachulish to sail up the Caledonian Canal to Inverness and heard it being said that the first shot had been fired. I remember that the closeness of the dark water to the cabin windows was awesome and at Inverness I clearly remember riding to the railway station in a cab. We arrived at my grandparent's house in the country to find that the war had touched them already. One of my uncles had already joined his regiment, The Black Watch, and the son of the neighbouring farmer had ridden their fine farm horse 'Joubert' to Elgin to take their place with The Scottish Horse.

It was from this place in the country that parcels of butter and eggs and fruit came to town to help us through the war, and helped my father to a new hobby very different to his reserved occupation of keeping the City supplied with electricity. The land behind our back gardens and Craigie Loanings was waiting for what is now Craigie Park to be built. It was sheltered by the high wall of Hamilton Place Lane. We had seen an old man digging beside this wall and now allotments were available there, and my father ventured to take one. He enlisted the help of his friend and foreman at the Electricity Works - a countryman who knew all about cultivating a garden and between them they grew great crops. There was a ploy when he sent empty jam jars for my mother to use the lovely country fruit at her home to fill with jam for our winter. He packed them one year with his special green peas to impress his father-in-law - alas the jars were late in being collected and his wonderful peas had perished. For a time gorgeous fruit from country gardens were carefully picked and packed and sent from stations all down the Highland railway line to be sold next day in Edinburgh shops.

In 1915 I went to the Aberdeen High School for Girls, whose motto was 'By Learning and Courtesy'. Because the school buildings in Albyn Place had been requisitioned my first days at school were spent at 7 Queens Gardens at Queens Cross, and later at Queens Cross Church Hall. I think most of our classes were of about 40 pupils.

We had a brilliant first teacher who had us learning tables and maths essentials that were props for life. There were good schools in town where girls had a much wider range of jobs. It is interesting to think how it was in the country. My mother was a governess when she married. She had been through the village school and won a bursary to go on to the Academy in the next town. This was a good education and she and others could have gone on to higher things, but they cost too much. However as the daughter of a known local family she was suitable for a 'Big House' where they were looking for

Above: Teenage fashion in the late nineteenth century, all made by a lady in a country cottage near the Moray Coast.

a governess. Later she moved to London and Glasgow. Over the centuries, sewing had been a necessary accomplishment and both my mother and her mother went to classes at the nearest town, where the main drapery employed a resident dressmaker who was called - in my mother's case - a 'Court dressmaker', but in Charles Murray's poem 'The Packman' she was a 'Quine taken in to sew.'

When I left school I worked as a dress designer and cutter with a small workroom of dressmakers whose work was exquisite. Girls who did domestic work in a big well-staffed house came away with a variety of careers, but the lassie who went young and raw to the farm kitchen or general domestic service in town may have had a rougher time.

It was not so very long since the piano had become an important part of country as well as town houses, and girls were expected to play. For one thing churches were very active and choir singing was very much a part of the services, with anthems and solos in different denominations. The choir and choir practices were part of social life and continued as part of social evenings in private houses at home. My father and his brothers were very musical and I can still hear echoes of 'I hear you calling me' and other drawing-room ballads. There were amateur operettas too, and I well remember an evening at the Beach Pavilion where I was taken when very young when a friend was singing there. The regular stars there were a very popular husband and wife called Violet Davidson and Davy Thomson. Two of their songs were 'You are my honeysuckle - I am the bee', and 'You great big beautiful doll.' They had a variety of stars at the Pavilion and eventually the great Harry Gordon and there was always the gramophone at home. During the wars there were a great number of amateur productions all getting very good audiences, and I believe more stimulating on both sides of the curtain than all today's armchair 'Soaps'. Early visits to His Majesty's Theatre were great events, especially in far away days when the first pantomime I saw was Cinderella and no modern T.V. animation can rival 'Peter Pan',

with children like ourselves flying in rooms like our own and out of the window into the night. Another show which gave great entertainment all round was the student's Gala Week revue for charity. This took place at the end of the Easter vacation.

My school friend Rita Chapman had organised splendid historical costumes for a performance of 'Town and Gown' and invited me to join her in the first revue on His Majesty's stage. This required maximum effect with minimum expense, and was mainly achieved then with the help of one of Aberdeen's great shops of the time - 'Raggy Morrisons', where Marks & Spencers is now. Raggys dealt in bankrupt stock and was full of a variety of good clothes, at reasonable prices. We were puzzled about one scene in which we had to dress in bright winter jerseys till we went round to Raggys, who were advertising men's 'semmets' (undervests) selling for 6d each. Some packets of dyes and a touch of

Programme cover for the student production at His Majesty's Theatre - 1947, and a page of adverts from the programme.

BROWNE
-41

individual designing and we had our scene saved!
The great event of the 20s was the coming of wireless. My father was fascinated by the technical possibilities of this new medium, but not everyone appreciated it. My father was visiting an elderly neighbour and telling him about this new marvel, but one old gentleman who was also there turned to the other and said "Ah, wireless - a passing phase"! These words were spoken in Beechgrove House, until recently home of the BBC, Aberdeen. The original BBC studio in Aberdeen was in the basement of Mr Botting's shop 'The Aberdeen Electrical Engineering Company' in Belmont Street. I still have the little crystal set which was put in the middle of a card table while the listeners sat round attached to earphones listening to 'Toy Town' and 'The Brain's Trust' and some good programmes produced locally from 2BD

Above: Queens Cross, Aberdeen circa 1929. Nannie Thomson and Rita Chapman as two 'French Maids/Nurses', with Stephen Mitchell as 'Baby'. The policeman is real!

Left: More adverts from the Students Revue programme, this time it's the 1947 show.

Facing page: Programme cover for the student production at His Majesty's Theatre - 1941.

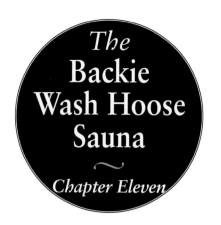
Flora Duncan

Flora's photographs reach far back to the late 1780s. Having arrived from Cromarty and the Clearances her ancestors settled to a new life in the area surrounding New Deer. The house they lived in was called *'Mid Old What'* and was superseded by the house built on its old foundations by Charles Henderson and Mary Jane Murdoch, who were Flora's grandparents. Called *'Oldwhat'* this house, built in 1900, becomes the point from which the seven children, one of whom was Flora's mother Jeanie, began their lives. We watch through these photographs and reminiscences, the dynasty traversing the decades to the 1960s and the birth of Flora's last child Colin.

<u>Flora Duncan:</u> This is the earliest photograph that we have. This man was my great great grandfather. His name was William Murdoch and he was a farmer in New Deer. Born in 1782, he was married to Mary Finnie at New Deer in 1824.

<u>Facing page:</u> This is me taken in 1939, I was four at the time.

Trevor: It looks as though your family were quite well off.

Flora: Well both sides were well off, m' grandfather on my father's side was a cattle breeder. His name was John McGregor Petrie and had a farm called

Mains of Asleid near New Deer. He nearly always won the first prize for his Aberdeen Angus cattle and he used t' go to Buenos Aires and give lectures about cattle rearing. All his cattle got exported there. However durin' the First World War he was unable to export his cattle and that finished him. On my mother's side there were farmers as well but it was the endowment from her uncle's estate which made her well off.

Top: Here we have John R. Murdoch born 1859. He was the half-brother of my grandmother's and he became a rich man. He went to Assam in India and became a tea planter there. He left the family £10,000 when he died. This money was to be divided between my granny's seven children.

Centre: This is the marriage of my grandfather and grandmother at 21 Broomhill Road. The groom Charles Henderson stands fifth from the left, and the bride, Mary Jane Murdoch, is centre with the bouquet. The photograph was taken in June 1896. My great grandfather Sandy Duncan sits below the drying pole.

Bottom: This is William Murdoch, who was born in 1827 and was the son of the William Murdoch pictured on the previous page. He is seen here with his wife Jane Mackie who came from New Pitsligo where she was a milliner. Her father, George Mackie, born 1795 was a master shoe-maker of 123 High Street, Ellon.

Far left: My father with one of m' grandad's bulls at Mains of Asleid. These bulls were sold abroad for breeding.

That's my mother Jeannie sitting next to my grandmother who was born in 1867. The first born, my uncle rests on the knee of my grandfather Charles Henderson. That uncle eventually went to Australia.

My father was top herdsman at his father's farm but there was a disagreement between him and his father who then put him away from the farm. This was at the time of the depression and there was no work to be had so they came into Aberdeen and rented a flat that was an attic at 28 Jasmine Terrace. My father died at the age of 37 and my mother was left with five of a family. He died of peritonitis in the hospital at Woolmanhill. He was wounded in the First World War and the shrapnel had entered his bloodstream. That was in 1936 when I was four months old, therefore I never knew him. So she had quite a handful. Seven of us lived in this one attic and that's where I was born. Things were very cramped and my sister said that she slept in a kist. My mother now was living in poverty after being a rich woman, whilst the rest of her family were well off. My mother was then widowed when I was four months old and we continued to live at Jasmine Terrace till a council house became available in Woodside.

This is the family later on when there were seven children. Uncle John (far right) he turned out to be quite famous. He was a composer and produced a well known book of music. His daughter Esther, next to my grandmother is still living. She is 92 (2000) a retired schoolteacher and a spinster.

1. Here is my mother Jeanie Henderson aged 18 and the other photo depicts her two sisters, Mary and Esther. Esther is still alive today (2000)

2. This is the earliest photograph I have of my father, Jack Petrie. It was taken when he was three or four in 1901.

3. This photograph shows the new family house which was built in 1900 in the parish of New Deer. Called 'Nether Old What' the house was built on the old foundations of the family's previous home called 'Mid Old What'. This ancient house had a thatched roof and some of it was constructed of heather and whin. It was in this house that William died in 1867 and Flora's mother was born in 1897. Three years later the new house was built. It shows my grandparents Mary Jane Murdoch, and Charles Henderson with their first three children, left to right Charlie, Jeannie (Flora's mother) and William. In the doorway is Flora's great great grandmother, Christina Smith. She brought my grandfather up as my great grandmother had remarried.

4. Here is my father Jack Petrie at Robert Gordon's where he was boarded and educated. Third from the left, front row. That was taken before the First World War broke out.

5. Here he is at 21. He was commissioned and this shows him as a Lieutenant in the Gordon Highlanders. Although he was wounded he got back alive and became top herdsman at his father's farm.

I was brought up in Woodside and I went to Kittybrewster School. My brother was Dux of Frederick Street School and my sister Gladys went there as well because they all lived in Jasmine Terrace. Esther my mother's sister, went to King Street School. Eventually, when we moved to Woodside they went to Powis School. My father, before he died at the early age of 37, had a job on a coalboat unloading coal at the harbour. This was felt as a come-down for the family. We didn't get much of a chance in life because my mother didn't have any money to educate us. It helped a bit when m' brother became Dux and my sister Gladys won a bursary. She was sent out to my grandmother's to help on the farm in the summer holidays which meant that it was one less

Above left: This is my parent's wedding. They were married at New Deer in 1922.

Above: I was married to William Duncan in 1956. With me is Esther my sister and on the left was m' husband's brother-in-law. Bill, my husband was a corporal in the Seaforth Highlanders. He was then immediately posted to Gibraltar.

Left: That's me on the left, aged 11 with my friend Dorothy.

Above: Taken at the Bay of Nigg on a picnic. That's me bottom right with Jean and behind are my two older sisters Gladys and Esther.

Above right: This is my mother's aunt, Maggie Duncan. She is also on my granny's wedding photograph.

mouth for my mother t' feed. M' granny gave my mother £1 for Glady's help. Generally we didna get a chance and we felt missed out. Mother got 25 shillings (£1.25) a week. She got 10 shillings (50p) for herself after she was widowed and she got three shillings (15p) each for her family. My mother never went out, she never left us and she was a first class mother. She would sit and knit or sew for us but financially she was held down right to the end. She was never out of her kitchen baking and she could make a meal out of nothing.

I always remember at Christmas time, I was always cryin' because I believed in Santa. It was Hogmanay that we hung up our stocking not Christmas. There was me cryin' on New Year's mornin' because Santa didn't bring me what the other children got. My friend, whose father was a sergeant major in the army, she used t' get dolls and prams an' that from Santa whilst my sister and I would run to the mantelpiece for our stockings but we'd be lucky if we got an apple or an orange. We'd cry asking, "What did we do? Santa didn't bring us a doll." When we went out there were the children with all their toys and we had got an orange and an apple. Of course our mother did her best but we didn't understand at the time.

Trevor: So what did you do when you left school?

Flora: I went out to work in Balgownie Dairy in George Street at the household grocery department. I wanted to be a hairdresser or a gym teacher but my mother couldn't afford the fees. You had to pay the fees three months in advance but we hadn't the money, and our mother couldn't wait till we went out to work so that we could contribute. My sister Jean, she ended up in a baker's shop whilst I went to the wholesale grocery.

I had several boyfriends. We used to go to the dancin'; the Palais and the Milburn. Later I met my husband at the Palais; the dance hall in Diamond Street. At the time he had just come back from Aden, that was at the end of 1955 and we were married in June 1956 just before the beginning of the Suez Crisis. I then had my first child, Billy, and although I had married quarters at Fort George for two months my husband was soon off to Gibraltar where he was stationed for Suez, so I went back to live with my mother. When he came back we were stationed in Munster in Germany where Terry was born. We then went to Aldershot for two years and from there we went to Singapore from 1961 to '64. Colin, my third son was born there in 1962.

My children Terry, Colin and Billy.

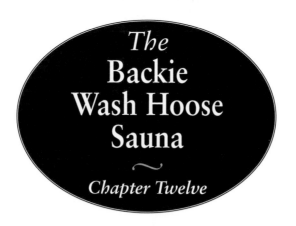

Emma Webster

111 *Bon Accord Street was both the centre of Mrs Webster's young life and also later in life when she returned from living in Glasgow, London and America, she bought the family house and refurbished it to suit her needs. With a nostalgic view of yester-year Mrs Webster's vignette is a delightful memoir of a young life lived in a secure home environment. However, America became an important part of her life - both her brothers were sent there to find a better life. Mrs Webster herself also visited America and stayed for several years, whilst later, her three daughters emigrated to the United States.*

Main picture: Emma Webster.

Inserts: Top/centre - Exterior and interior photographs of Campbell's the undertakers, at the top of Bon Accord Street.
Bottom - Emma's house at No.111 Bon Accord Street.

Mrs Webster: My father was an Aberdonian and we lived in Bon Accord Street. We had a whole house in those days.

Trevor: So what did your father do for a living?

Mrs Webster: He was a postie, but actually he was the King's Messenger and was sent to Balmoral; he was very proud of that. I remember quite well him doing that, I was a schoolgirl at the time. He felt very grand as he had a railway carriage to himself. He had a lot of mail for the King and Queen which was carried in a special bag with the mail in it.

Trevor: How often would that have happened then?

Mrs Webster: Well, he went every day when the Royal Family were in residence at Balmoral. However, I couldn't be completely sure about it.

Top: That's my father and mother and those are my two brothers born before me. Their names were Harry and Dave and they both went to America. My mother's people went to America that's why my brothers went. It would have been another four years before I was born.

Above: This is my father in the 1880s seated second from the right. He was in the post office and was the King's Messenger.

I went to Ferryhill School and although I was good at English I was not much good at maths. I then went on to Ruthrieston School. I left school at 14 and got a job. I can't remember what it was but I had to get to a certain stage before I could become a telephone operator.

I passed the exam alright and then went on to work on the phone switchboard for about four years. I really enjoyed that job because there were a lot of girls and thus a choice of friends. Often we would run down to our house which was about 200 yards away from the Exchange. The girls used to come and I had a little flat at the top of the house. It was all very nice. We used to go to Lossiemouth for our

holidays. A taxi would take us with all our luggage down to the station in Aberdeen and then we'd be off to Lossiemouth by train. My mother came from Lossiemouth you see, but she had no relatives there because they had gone to America and her mother went to America.

Trevor: You said earlier that your brothers went to America when they were young, is that who they went to?

Mrs Webster: Yes they did go but the Wall Street Crash of 1929 occurred and there was no work for anyone. Harry went to the Hoover Dam when it was being constructed and helped to build that. Well they had to do something. I went to see my brothers there eventually and as I said, stayed there for a couple of years.

Above: I worked at a telephone exchange. It was at the top of Bon Accord Street in those days. They were most of the girls from the Exchange. It was all manual in those days and you had to reach for all of the numbers. That's me 2nd from the left on the back row.

Trevor: It must have been difficult for you to have been estranged from your brothers at such an early age. How did you cope with that?

Mrs Webster: My mother didn't like them leaving but she was glad for them because her mother was out there, and of course mother's family were great letter writers so I received many letters from them which helped a great deal. Harry eventually got his own business and Dave became a farmer.

Eventually I then got married and we moved to Bridge of Weir near Glasgow where my husband, who originally came from Arbroath, got a job at the head office of the Clydesdale Bank. We stayed there for a few years and then went to London with our three daughters, who are all in America now. Our home was in Epsom in Surrey and we stayed there for about 12 years where I looked after the home. He was just about to become the general manager when he took ill and died about a year later. After that I went to America for a couple of years and eventually I decided that I'd like to live in Aberdeen again. So I bought the family house at 111 Bon Accord Street, spent a lot of money getting it done the way I always wanted it. It was a four storey house and I made it into two flats, one in the basement and one on the next floor and then I had the two top floors with a balcony on the first floor. By this time my children had all grown up and had gone to America.

111 is opposite Bon Accord Crescent. I loved the old house and I got a wonderful man to come and do it. He had three other workers and he turned it into the most wonderful house and I let the two flats which gave me an income.

Trevor: When you first lived in that house, what was your life like? What sort of things did you do?

Mrs Webster: I was always out doing the usual things which young people did in those days. We often went to the Beach Ballroom or the Palais to the dances. I had a very happy home life where everything was stable, which is important for a girl of 14.

Trevor: Tell me about some of the things that you remember about your childhood.

Mrs Webster: Well, when I was about nine years old I remember looking in at the open back door of Pat Magee, the tailor's shop, where four or five men sat cross-legged, 'sewing suits for gentlemen'. Sitting on a very large table! I think it came to my mind as I went to the 'Jint Station' and saw new buildings where the shop had been, at the end of Bridge Street, and round the corner. This brings to mind the wooden bridge, long gone, down that street called Windmill Brae and over to The Green under Union Bridge, dark with lime stalactites, then along Denburn, where we found swings. That's where I slipped off, and it came back and hit me, bang! On my head. I have never been the same since!

I bought a bell in Aberdeen sometime ago, not an ordinary bell, but one that would have been set ringing when someone opened the door into the little shop next door. It reminded me of when I gazed through the window where lucky tatties and 'soda fountains' (with two banana sweeties) gave us a choice for the ha' penny we meant to spend. The tatties nearly always won, for there was always the gamble that "wi'd find inside another ha'penny. " Now the little shop is a turf accountant. The bell could easily have been one of the five bells above the scullery door in our kitchen which over a century ago summoned the little maid to build up the fire in the parlour, or in my day, to answer the front door. They were happy days when no one had invented potato crisps or coke, and we were very content. On Sundays we spent the day in the parlour, and had tea on a lovely oval table. We sat on the sofa and two armchairs. My brothers hadn't much time for all this fuss, and had fun shouting up and down 'the lock' which was a speaking tube through which, in the earlier days, the little maid had been ordered to bring up the meal! I had been heard to say, "I want to go home" for our kitchen with its shining range was home, and we could toast our own bread by the fire. On Saturday nights my mother and father went out, and the boys had a whale of a time with their friends, but when they heard the front door open, they all sat down, all sticking their chewing gum under their chairs.

My father was a football fan and, though he was a quiet man, he came home quite hoarse, shouting for 'the Dons'. He always stopped at the Castlegate and brought home coconut ice, pear drops and Swiss milk toffee, and we sat by the kitchen-grate and munched away happily until they had all gone. I remembered the horses' hooves clattering on the cassies past our windows, as Dr Ogilvy-Will set off on his rounds, at eight a.m. on the dot, down the road from Campbell's where 20 or 30 horses were stabled. What a sight it was to see them prancing down the ramp, for their stalls were up in the gallery above the big enclosed yard; especially the big black funeral horses, with their feathery plumes tossing, waiting to be hitched to the hearse.

Now the cobbles have been torn up by a monster earth-mover and the old granite paving sent off to be laid in the Winter Gardens in the Duthie Park. I wonder why we must always destroy in the name of progress? We never can replace the history that goes with it.

**Photographs courtesy of
William Gilchrist, Funeral
Directors, Aberdeen.**

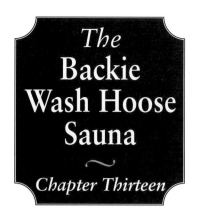

The Backie Wash Hoose Sauna

Chapter Thirteen

Margaret Farquhar

Margaret outlines her life and her movement upwards from the modest position of clerical assistant, through the ranks to reach the heights of Lord Provost and the receipt of the CBE in 1998. As Lord Provost she had the common touch that gave her a humanity which was quite uncommon. She became the people's favourite, and will be remembered long after her retirement.

Above left: I was probably eight there. I think it was taken at one of the bowling greens and I think it was Albury, because my father enjoyed playing bowls and I suppose that we would have been with him.

Above right: This photo taken at Grainger's Studio in Holburn Street shows my mother and father and the two of us. I'm the young one, I'd have been about 12 or 14. Mother made all our clothes and these velvet dresses were no exception.

Facing page: This is my school photo when I was at Broomhill School.

Margaret: I was born in Aberdeen in Broomhill Road and I went to the primary school there and later to Ruthrieston. I left Ruthrieston School at 16 and had a year in Webster's College for shorthand and typing and bookkeeping. That was in Bon Accord Square. My mother paid to give us a year there, that was a college that was private to a certain extent but my mother had t' pay for our fees. She was determined that both my sister and I would become shorthand typists. However, I really wanted t' go into a shop because my aunt had a shop in Cuminestown out towards Turriff and it sold just about everything. I was fascinated by this little shop and we used t' go up there for our holidays. They had potatoes, vegetables, everything was there, from a needle to anything else that you wanted and they had petrol round the back.

Trevor: How come they were living there?

Margaret: Well, my father actually came from Strichen and my grandfather was a shepherd in that area so my father was

Above: This is m' granny MacIntosh and m' sister out at Chestnut Row which is just across the road from Berryden.

Left: I stayed in Broomhill Road and this is the next door neighbour's house. Here we have a concert party for the war effort. There's me, the child to the left of the lady with the specs. The old lady was known as Granny Gruer, she was well into her 90s when I got married. These are all kids who stayed just round about us. I think we made about £100 which was a lot of money in those days. I am standing in the 4th row from the front, 4th right. (Copyright Aberdeen Journals Limited.)

born there. He came into Aberdeen after that in between the wars about 1922-24. My mother and father were married and their first house was down in Dee Street. At that time you could buy not only the house but all the things in it. It cost about £200, a lot of money in those days! Cutlery, bedding everything and y' bought the whole lot. They then moved to 35 Broomhill Road in 1926. I stayed there till I was 21 when I got married.

Trevor: What did your dad do for a job?

Margaret: He worked for the North of Scotland Electricity Company at that time. He was a

Top: Here we see my grandparents. He was a shepherd just out past Ellon. Burnett was the family name. The photograph was taken at Midstocket Road.

Above: That's the back green of 35 Broomhill Road where I stayed and we used t' come down the stairs there. That's my mother and my grandfather.

Left: This is my father when he was in the army during the First World War. He was a Royal Artillery Linesman.

meter inspector and he had a motorbike and he had t' travel out t' Culter from where he worked. He was there for 35 years. He got extra money for travelling but eventually they took him back into Millburn Street where the head office was. His salary was reduced by about five shillings less than m' sister was getting in a secretarial job. Although I went into the college for shorthand and typing I didn't like shorthand and I was more interested in the bookkeeping. My first job I had was with the North of Scotland College of Agriculture at 41½ Union Street but I only stayed there for about nine months before I left to work for Charles Michie the haulage contractor in Richmond Street. I was there from 18 to 21 when I got married.

I finished work then because in those days you stayed at home after you got married. That was June 1951. We had one room in Crown Street on the corner of Affleck Street - a cold brute of a room in the winter time. The toilet was out in the lobby and there was a little wash-hand basin there as well. There was the wash house downstairs where you got most of your water. For heating we used an electric fire and we only had a grill to cook everything on and there was no oven. Billy my son was born there but by the time I had Hazel we got a council house up on North Anderson Drive. I thought it was great and that all m' Christmases had come together.

Six weeks after we'd got married my husband lost his job and it took two or three weeks for him to find one, so things were a bit tight at that time. He was a baker by trade and he used t' work up at Reid's the bakers in Rosemount. He more

Top: My father, Donald Burnett, was a football trainer and you can see him here on the extreme right with the towel. The football team was called The Gallowgate UFFC in the early 20s.

Centre: This is even earlier when my father was playing but I don't remember what the team was. He is at the back, second from the left.

Bottom: This was the Allotment Association's Prize Giving and this is Lady Tweedsmuir presenting a trophy to my father who had his allotment across from Broomhill School. (Copyright Aberdeen Journals Limited.)

or less took over the place because the owner was not that well. However before that, he was injured. He was making butter biscuits and he put his fingers through the break rollers whilst mixing the dough. He didn't lose any fingers, although two of them were damaged and he had very little feeling in his thumb. He returned to work but the ligaments in his arm were damaged and he was advised to find something else. He then got a job down at the beach as a life saver for the summer season, with the understanding that if there was a vacancy at the swimming pool he would get it. The following year he got a permanent job and from there he went up to the Bon Accord Baths. After that he went to the University swimming pool, teaching students swimming. After a few years there he got a job out at Linn Moor for disabled children and was there for about 10 years until he retired because of ill health.

Trevor: When did you go back to work then?

Margaret: When Hazel was about eight I took a morning job at Cordiner's in Sinclair Road, who were box makers at that time and I was in the offices there for a while. That was from nine till one but as the children didn't want school dinners any longer I packed that in. During the 1960s they were in their teens and were at Northfield Academy so they could look after themselves. I then went to work part-time for William Walker's Transport in

Top: This is before we got married. We were just going together at that time. I put the picture into one of the weekly magazines and we won a five bob prize for it!

Above: That's my son Billy with my mother and father at Aikey Fair.

Persley. He only had about two lorries and he sort of paid his drivers out of his pocket. PAYE was just coming in so I had to start off the business there with books and sort out the tax and things like that. I was there for about eight years when I started with the council, but I worked part-time for William Walker for about five years after that. He was a very good boss who often gave me time off when I needed it. I found it very difficult at that time because I had

123

become a magistrate and I was a fortnight in every 12 weeks on the bench. So when I got home at night I was absolutely shattered. So I then left Walker's and by this time he had about 10 vehicles.

Trevor: How did you become a magistrate?

Margaret: It was the councillors who chose the magistrates and they asked me if I would like to become one. I didn't really know what it entailed but then I often said yes to things before I realised what it entailed! There were six magistrates at the council at that time and I was the fifth. You then moved up from there. The magistrate's work was mostly court work then but today this work is executed by the justices in District Court. There were magistrates in the 60s when I started before I came onto the council. I started in '71 and in '75 it all changed. They did away

And here are the four of us together with Billy and Hazel at the back. March 1981.

with the magistrates and they brought in the justices who took over the court work. It was small things like small traffic offences and drunkenness I dealt with but

today it's getting much more serious. As a magistrate I generally dealt with offenders in a sympathetic way, but when they had spent all the money on alcohol when there was a wife and children at home, that riled me a bit. The difficulty was that if you fined them the family suffered yet again.

Trevor: I suppose that is why the mother got paid Family Allowance later on.

Margaret: Yes that was really what was changed but there were the frequent offenders who were often drunk and incapable. They were often taken in for a while, dried out and put out again. They would often meet you in the street and greet y' with "Fit like Your Honour." They haven't the money and it's just a waste o' time. Occasionally they would get drunk on purpose just t' get prison for a while especially over Christmas.

During the first two years as a magistrate I also became a convener of one of the small committees which was for Housing and General Purposes. I did that for about six months before they reorganised it all in 1974. The Council was then split into the District Council and the Regional Council. At that time they had just started with the DLO - the Direct Labour Organisation which was supposed t' be separated from the council work and run itself. I then became convener of the Works Department as it was called then. I progressed on from there to the Environmental Health and Cleansing. It was a progression but y' didn't think of it in that way. For instance, one of the things that every councillor did when they were first elected was to put in for any committees you fancied to serve on. Often councillors would make adjustments so that you could get the committees that you wanted. I tried to try all the committees and there was only one that I didn't get on to which was 'Personnel' and I was not that keen about that one anyway. Eventually I got on to Planning and I was there about eight years. Then I got onto Finance; it was part of policy and resources. My work there was as Policy Convener but I had finance to deal with. Unfortunately, Tom Paine who was the convener for policy took a stroke, so I had to step up into the policy convener's job which I found difficult but I managed. Reorganisation took place in '95. We had no finances the first year, we just had t' set up policies and I was convener of that. There was no Lord Provost because Jim Wyness had another year to go until he ended his four year period but in 1996 I was made Lord Provost then.

Trevor: How did y' feel about that, could you see it coming?

Margaret: For the last three elections I had been asked by some of the members if I would like to be Provost and I said, "Well, put my name forward". I just thought that having the interviews and the run up to it was experience for me and never thinking that I would get on but they were determined that there was going to be a woman Lord Provost and so I became the first woman to fill the post.

Top: Here's me standing in for the Provost, see the little chain I have on. It was for a Girls Brigade AGM in 1979.

Above: At the gates of Buckingham Palace. Here I am with my daughter showing off my CBE. It was a proud moment for me, it certainly was.

Left: In her official photo, The Lord Provost looks grand in her regalia.

Schools' Project

This cross-generational project is a collaboration between Aberdeen City Council's Arts Development Team and Oral History Project, and funded by the Great Northern Partnership. Some older people were invited to Smithfield and Kittybrewster Primary Schools to be interviewed about their lives by a primary six or seven class as an intergenerational programme. Here below are a part of those interviews. We thank those schools for their willing co-operation in the scheme.

Kittybrewster Primary School interviewees:

Flora Duncan
Mrs Duff and
Lord Provost Margaret Smith.

Daniel: Where and when were you born?

Mrs Duff: I was born in Port Gordon in 1918.

Rebecca: Did you enjoy your time at school?

Mrs Duff: Yes, I went to the High School in Buckie but I was brought up in Port Gordon and I went to the primary school there before I shifted to Buckie.

Cameron: Did you get the strap?

Mrs Duff: Oh no I was never so bad as that, but there were plenty who did get it.

   The teachers were all very nice but some of them had a strap and some of them had a cane in case someone was naughty, and if y' got that your hand would get blisters.

Christopher: How have things changed since you were at school?

Mrs Duff: There is a lot more freedom compared to my days at school. They were very strict with us when we were young.

Nicholas: In what way were they strict?

Mrs Duff: Well, you had to pay attention and y' hadn't to speak in the classroom.

Michaela: We work in groups in our school now, so we have to talk.

Mrs Duff: Yes but we had to work by ourselves using a slate to write on.

Grace: The difference is amazing, we can even use a computer to write with these days.
  But did you have to say things like times tables out loud?

Mrs Duff: Yes we had to do that, do you have to?

Grace: No we just do it in a book and write down the answer.

Shelley: Do you think that it was better when you were at school?

Mrs Duff: Yes, you had t' tell the teacher the answer and if you made a mistake you had to do it again. Our school bags were made out of sailcloth and they cost a shillin' (5p) each.

Callum: What sort of desk did you sit at?

Mrs Duff: It was one of those ones with inkwells in the desk and had a seat attached.

Neil: Did you take school dinners?

Mrs Duff: There were no school dinners. I used t' go home for mine because I lived close to the school. If you lived in the country you would have to take a packed lunch. They'd come in with their flask and oatcakes. They were very poor times in those days.

Dean: What sort of transport did you have then?

Mrs Duff: We had no transport. We had to walk everywhere.

Daniel: Would you like to go back to those times?

Mrs Duff: No, no, they were very poor times and we had t' work very hard for our money at that time. However, we were very content even though we were poor. People get too much these days and they never seem contented.

Zoe: How old were you when you left school and did you have to get a job straight away?

Mrs Duff: Most of us left at 14 and we then got a job. I became a servant in a big house and they were very, very hard on you. I worked in the house and fed the chickens. I'd light the fires in the kitchen and the livingroom then go upstairs and clean that one out. It was very hard work but when I was 17 I passed a medical so that I could work on the buses. I started with a small company to begin with, Miller was his name but eventually Alexander's bought him out.

Amanda: When you lived in Port Gordon how often did you come in to Aberdeen?

Mrs Duff: I never came in to Aberdeen because we never had enough money to pay for the fare.

Mark: Did you ever go on holiday?

Mrs Duff: No not in those days, but I've been on holiday more recently.

Pauline: Do you get buckies from Buckie?

Mrs Duff: Yes you found them along the shore. Buckie was a fishing village and the fishermen all went away to Yarmouth at this time o' year but there's nothing o' that now. They filled the barrels o' herrin' and sent it to Russia.

Michael: Is Buckie a big place?

Mrs Duff: It is quite a big place now but it was just a village in my day.

Shelley: Do you remember the war and was it scary?

Mrs Duff: Yes and it was. A bomb went off in Portknockie and it ruined the school and went down Admiralty Street and killed a number of people there.

Rebecca: Were they friends of yours?

Mrs Duff: No, but I knew them because I worked on the buses up and down the coast so I knew pretty much everybody.

Daniel: Which bus did you work on then?

Mrs Duff: Macduff to Inverness.

Neil: Why did you come to bide in Aberdeen?

Mrs Duff: Well, it was because my husband worked in Aberdeen.

Grace: When you were a child what did you have for Christmas?

Mrs Duff: We didna get much in the way of toys but we might get a doll and an orange and an apple put into y' stocking and a sweetie peg. At Christmas in Port Gordon every shop used t' put out oranges and apples at their door and they used t' throw them to the children. We used to put on big jumpers so that we could catch them! We used t' go from shop to shop 'shiving' we used to call it. There were two brothers and m' self and we started at the top o' the town and just walked right down till our jumpers couldna carry any more!

———

Sean: Where were you born?

Margaret: Near Leicester in England. My mother and father came from the Clyde near Glasgow so my blood is Scottish, and though I was born in England I consider myself Scottish.

Dean: What do you do as the Lord Provost?

Margaret: I am often there to represent Aberdeen City. For example I went to someone's 100th birthday party for a man from the city.

Nicholas Stephen: How did you become a councillor?

Margaret: Well, I became a councillor in 1988 and was in the political party that was in charge of the council. That was the Labour Party and in 1999 I was voted in by my colleagues in the Labour Party who were on the council.

Callum Stewart: What did you get for Christmas?

Margaret: I haven't thought about this for years but I remember getting a teddy bear, some dominoes and a lot of books.

Kristoffer: What was your first job?

Margaret: My first job was as a secondary teacher in physical education and English.

Callum: What was it like at your school?

Margaret: It was rather strange because I went to two primary schools and two secondary schools, which was rather confusing for me. The last school I went to was in Lancashire and it was called Southport High School for Girls.

Fraser: Did you get the belt at school?

Margaret: Yes I got the belt once. Those were the days when we got milk and it was little bottles and the top of the bottle was a piece of cardboard with a hole in it. Y' punched the hole out and you pulled the top off with the little hole. Now this little piece of card fell into the inkwell so I put the piece of cardboard on my hanky and to dry it out I whacked it up and down on the desk. Because I made a noise I got the belt.

Christopher Cook: Have you met the Queen?

Margaret: Yes, two months ago when she came up in an aeroplane to Aberdeen Airport to go to Balmoral.

Flora Duncan: I started at Kittybrewster School in 1940.

Cameron: What differences can you see from when you started to now in 1999?

Flora: The building is pretty much the same but in the classrooms y' had small desks with tops you could lift up and you kept all your books in there. There was an inkwell and a pen and there was a ridge across the desk to keep your pen.

Nicholas: Did you get the belt?

Flora: I got the belt once. When I was at school the teachers were very strict. In our classrooms the girls would be on one side and the boys the other and there were 48 children in the class. When y' were doing your lessons and the teacher was reading to you, or you were doing your sums or English, if you were distracted or started speaking to anyone the teacher would take the pad that she rubbed out the chalk on the blackboard and she would throw it at you. If it hit y' you went home with a bump and your mother said, "What's that on your head?" If you told her that the teacher had thrown the pad at you for speaking in class she would give you a tellin' off or a smack for misbehaving in the class.

Michaela: Did you ever get a ruler across your knuckles?

Flora: Yes, for speaking in the class. I got the strap once only. We had two playgrounds; one for the boys and one for the girls and one time I was in the boys' playground and I was sent to the headmaster and I got the strap for that. I never went into the boys' playground again!

Megan: What did you like doing at school?

Flora: I used to like going to highland dancin' and tap dancing. There was Scottish country dancin' as well, the Patronella and the Flowers of Edinburgh are two I remember.

You get an awful lot more chances today. We were quite poor and didn't get much help from the government - I wanted to be a hairdresser or a gym teacher and because my mother was very poor she couldn't educate me by sending me on to college. My mother had five o' a family and my father had died when I was a small child so she couldn't afford anything like that. You have much better opportunities today.

Zoe: After Kittybrewster did you go to Powis?

Flora: Yes and that was a very good school. When I lived in Woodside it was totally different because y' had no traffic on the roads when I was at school. There were no cars and there were lots of horses and carts so the roads were very easy to cross to get to school.

Amanda: Were the trams slow as well?

Flora: The trams were very slow and there was a tram stop just up the road by the side o' St. Machar Drive and there was another at the Northern Hotel.

Pauline: I'm not sure that I want t' go to St Machar Academy because they say y' get a first year hidin'.

Flora: Oh I don't think so, that's just to frighten you because the teachers nowadays would not allow that sort of thing to happen.
  You've a lot to thank Kittybrewster School for today because we didn't have the luxuries like television and computers when I was here.

Michael: Where did you go to play after school?

Flora: Westburn Park, I used to walk from St. Machar's with m' friends up Lesley Road to the park. Or' if it was a sunny day we'd go down to the beach.

Mark: What sort of toys did you play with?

Flora: We had very little in the way of toys. See at Christmas time, my mother, as I told you was very, very poor and my sister and I, we used t' hang up our stockings and in those days we had coal fires and my mother had two elephants on the mantelpiece under which we put our stockings. This was not Christmas, it was on Hogmanay and we were hoping for dolls, little tea-sets and prams. So when we wakened up, we went over to the mantelpiece where we found a wee lump of coal which was for luck, an orange, an apple and a hanky. Some of our friends got dolls and things like that because they were a bit better off than us. We wondered what we had done wrong not to have got better things, but when we were older we realised why. However, our mother gave us a lot of love and affection which more than made up for the things we didn't have.

Smithfield Primary School interviews*

* Because of the experimental nature of the project the taped interviews made at Smithfield School were found to be too difficult to transcribe and therefore have not been included. We apologise to the children for this but we have included some photographs below and the names of those who took part.

Acknowledgements

Trevor Davies: Writer, Compiler and Interviewer
Bill Smith: Designer
Andrew Mitchell and **Amy Fraser:** Proof Readers and Publicity
David Atherton: Team Leader

Special thanks to:
Valerie Plante: Genealogical Research
Mike Dey and **Catherine Walker:** Aberdeen Maritime Museum
Jim Pratt: Aberdeen Central Library
Jill Bauld: Arts Development Officer
Frank Donnelly: Planning & Strategic Development
Malcolm Dow: William Gilchrist, Funeral Directors

We are grateful for the assistance of: **Aberdeen Journals Limited**

P6 Kittybrewster Primary School

**Amanda Kuzmicki / Callum Stewart / Callum Sutherland
Cameron Allan / Christopher Cook / Daniel O'Leary
Dean Sangster / Fraser Turnbull / Grace Ritchie
Kristopher White / Mark Littlejohn / Megan Gilchrist
Michael Mitchell / Michaela Forbes / Neil Rettie
Nicholas Ferguson / Nicholas Stephen / Pauline McCrae
Rebecca Munro / Sean Rocha / Shelley Muir
Zoe King**

P6/7 Smithfield Primary School

**Amanda Johnston / Charmaine D'Arcy / Charmaine Thomson
Claire Wallace / Cyndi McLeod / Danielle Watt
Darren O'Henley / James Smith / Jay Cunningham
John McPhee / Kerry Merchant / Kimberly McIntosh
Kimberley Shand / Laura MacIntyre / Liam Gove
Michaela Wood / Natasha Howie / Paul Monro
Raymond Hipson / Richard Stewart / Ryan Henderson
Shirley McDonald**

**Jim & Margaret Matthews
Mollie Beattie
Mima Skinner**

The Backie Wash Hoose Sauna

1. Mary Johnston (p49). This is her sister and husband posing with their friend, Jean Lockart.

2. Ina Ross (p21). Her father-in-law, Bill Ross (right), worked on the trams all his life. Seen here on the Bridge Street - Bay of Nigg run.

3. Shuttle Lane, a long since gone area of the East end. The main buildings are now the Whitespace Arts Workshops.

4. Friend of Jane Robertson (Mary Johnston p49), taken in Albyn Lane, 1927.

5. Flora Duncan (p105). Her maternal grandfather's two sisters, Mary Ann and Tina Henderson

ABERDEEN
CITY COUNCIL